Divine Intervention

Patricia Milner

©2008
Nightengale Press
A Nightengale Media LLC Company

Divine Intervention
Copyright ©2008 by Patricia Milner
Cover Design ©2008 by Nightengale Press

For information about Nightengale Press please
visit our website at www.nightengalepress.com.
Email: publisher@nightengalepress.biz
or send a letter to:
Nightengale Press
10936 N. Port Washington Road. Suite 206
Mequon, WI 53092
Library of Congress Cataloging-in-Publication Data

Milner, Patricia,
DIVINE INTERVENTION/ Patricia Milner
ISBN:1-933449-70-5
ISBN 13: 978-1933449-70-8
Memoir

Copyright Registered: 2008
First Published by Nightengale Press in the USA

November 2008

10 9 8 7 6 5 4 3 2 1

Printed in the USA and the UK

Dedication

I have written this book to help people heal: to know that it's all right to be different from others, and to have visions and experiences that many people never have in their entire lifetime. It's a privilege and honour to have insight and compassion for those who are not as fortunate as we are.

I want to dedicate this book to my father, Robert Milner, who was a very special influence in my life. He was an extraordinary person who, although he experienced a great deal of trauma, remained the exceptional person that he was. He had a short life, passing at the age of sixty-two years, but he was very special to my sister Angela, my brother Terry, my mother Ada, and especially to me.

Endorsement

Patricia Milner writes in a way that will ensure the reader is walking with her every step of her journey towards remembrance. Readers feel her pain and frustration of being a gifted healer and medium yet find themselves immersed in her triumphs and exaltation of her soul. Patricia has opened her heart and bared her soul so that others may be able to grasp the reality of a multidimensional universe where all humans are divinely connected.

Patricia takes her readers into a world where there is no death and shows them that with no true awareness there is no life. This book is not just a story about another medium, this book is a work of art, no different than a canvas full of color waiting to be interpreted by the observer. Nor is this book merely a compilation of events. It is soon to become a classic of a modern day heroine brave enough to be herself in a world that forgot the power of one voice.

Through Patricia's commitment to honor her own truth she is now helping thousands of others to find the power of their own voices.

Reverend Cherise Thorne
Founder of The Temple Of Knowing Spirit
www.knowingspirit.org

Acknowledgements

It never ceases to amaze me how the perfect people are put across our pathway at just the right time. I had only written magazine articles before I started this book. When I started writing, my fingers hit the keyboard and the words came tumbling out, straight from my heart.

I would like to give my sincere thanks to all those amazing people who contributed to this book. Without their support and guidance, my book would not have been published today.

I must have driven everyone barmy from the start. Without the support of my editors: Jackie L. Watts and Linda Woods, I would have never finished. Linda was a great inspiration to me by challenging my thoughts and questioning my doubts at the same time. She not only edited my book, but she helped me take it to print. Without Linda's help, I would have struggled and put the book aside.

And then, to find my dream publisher was truly inspirational. Valerie Connelly (Nightengale Press) has been an amazing support.

My brightest guiding light, though, was my father who told me that one-day, I would write a book. At seventeen, I laughed and said: "You must be joking." Well, Dad, you were right, as usual.

Having all these people on my side was a match made in heaven.

Here are two quotes that remain in my heart that I would like to share with you:

"I salute the light within your eyes where the whole universe dwells; for when you are at the centre within you, and I am at the place within me, we shall be one." Crazy Horse, Lakota.

"Everything on earth has a purpose, every person a mission." Morning Dove/Christine Quintasket Salish

PART ONE

Chapter One

Looking Back

*A*s I sit here in my healing room remembering and writing my life's journey (looking at how it was compared to how it is today), I have a strong sense of inner peace and knowing, like I've never felt before.

As I look around my room, I'm surrounded by my life's visions and experiences of colour, crystals, crystal mirrors, crystal singing bowls, light frequency and vibration. I have many fairies, angel ornaments, a dragon, an Indian, Buddha, Quan Chi and Merlin, Tiger, Indian and wolf pictures to keep me company. I also have a light system that can change the colour of my healing room. When I think of my early years, each chapter is a colour of red, blue, green, purple and yellow. Red, blue and purple are the predominate ones. Red is for anger and emotions. Purple for spirituality and my soul's journey. Blue for my healing and healing abilities. Also, finding my soul note and soul colour has helped me to understand my purpose in life and my soul's journey. It has not been an easy one, but it has made me who I am today. There is nothing that comes across my path now that I have not already experienced. It allows me to help people today and when I say I understand, it comes from the heart. I have truly experienced life and learned what I needed for my soul to grow.

Increasing our understanding of our journey and appreciating who we truly are, enriches our lives beyond measure. Our growth continues throughout life.

When we can learn from our experiences and change the patterns and blocks that we create, life can be more joyful and we can work towards its completion in the richest way possible.

Our capacity to influence and change the events and circumstances in our lives can best be understood by heightening our perception and sensitivities. The change is internal not external. We must want to change and make the change, rather than blame everything and everyone for something that is done to us. As I found out, the answer lies within me, not elsewhere.

Chapter Two

Early Years

*I*was born in Yorkshire, England in 1950 and remember my mother holding me for the first time. I thought: Who am I? What am I? Where am I? Why am I here? I watched people hover over me and say: "She is a very beautiful and special child. Look at those eyes and that smile." Behind their faces, I could see coloured lights moving around the room. They made me laugh. That's where I really wanted to be. Why couldn't I be there?

As early as three years old, I could sense people's feelings, emotions, fears, anger and frustration. I could hear their thoughts and know what they were going to say or do before they did. I could see colours around people, animals, trees and objects. When I touched things, they would change colour. I had visions about things that I did not understand until days/weeks/months later, when it would happen exactly as I had seen it. I saw beings and angels and travelled through time and space. I had out-of-body experiences. I did not understand why others could not see or do what I could do. I became afraid of what I could see, feel and hear. I would dream of a better time and I could visualise that better place where I wanted to be.

My early years were not easy. I was a young girl who had an older head on my shoulders than my years. I always felt like an outsider, searching for something and yet, did not know what I was searching for. In fact, I never felt that I belonged to anyone, any place, or even on the planet. I knew that I was here for a purpose, but what was it? People were wary of me so I never had any real friends.

No one understood me. I did not belong and did not feel loved. I felt isolated and so alone in a place I did not want to be. The only thing I had was my connection with animals. I seemed to be closer to them than people. I could speak to them through my mind and get answers back. I could give love to them and they would give it back, without question. No matter where I was, animals would be drawn to me.

My relationship with my mother was not good. I felt that she didn't love me because I couldn't be like my brother or sister. I was different. Because no one could understand me I became the rebel. I searched for love, attention and approval but never got it.

The one person I truly adored was my father. I loved him so much. I was so close to him but could not understand why. I just knew he was my hero. I didn't know, at the time, that my father would be a major influence and inspiration in my life.

Many times, in my early years, I thought I wanted to

end my life. The life experiences that I had, challenged me more and more and I had to deal with them on my own. I sometimes felt that I just couldn't take any more. I would push away the beings that tried to help me because I was angry. If I could see things and they were supposed to love me, why did they allow these things to happen to me?

In my early years, I experienced all the emotion any one could possibly have: fear, frustration, anger, lack of confidence and low self-esteem. I kept asking: Why me? I wrapped myself up with the visions and beings that I could see, until I lost faith in them. Then, I would push them away.

My mother said that I lived in a fantasy world and took me to the doctor. He said I would grow out of it. But here I am today and nothing has changed.

I knew that I was different. I used to love to find my own private space, where I could see other people. They would talk to me and make me feel special. The problem was, that no one else could see them. My mother said that they were my 'imaginary friends" and told me to go and join in with the rest of the family. The only problem was that I never felt like I was part of our family. I just felt that I didn't belong.

My father was a miner and my mother stayed at home to look after the kids. We lived at Highgate near Goldthorpe, Rotherham in South Yorkshire, England until I was three years old. Then, we moved to Thurnscoe, where we lived until I got married.

Mother and Father adored each other. Father was not a typical miner. He loved family life and never went out without my mother. We did things as a family.

Chapter Three

Close Encounters

As I grew older, I continued to hear voices and see my 'imaginary friends.' It happened more and more frequently and got stronger and stronger, especially when my mother and I were alone. At the age of four, Mother asked me: "Who are you talking to?" So, I told her: "It's Great Granddad and he wants to know if you remember your fourth birthday on George Street?'"

Mother freaked out because Great Granddad was dead. She told me that I had a problem and took me to the doctor right away.

The doctor took one look at me and said: "She has found an imaginary friend. When she goes to school she'll be fine. She will grow out of this."

There was a big discussion that night between my parents. They were looking at me but whispering in the corner so I could not hear. As they talked, voices came into my head: *Not to worry, everything will be fine.*

I tried to push those voices away because I felt that no one liked me because of them. The more I pushed against them, the more things happened.

I shared a bedroom with my sister, and in the evening, my mother would come, tuck us in, and say good-night. She would switch the light off as she went out the door, leaving it slightly open. I never opened my eyes in the dark, because I would see people. To hide from them, I would always sleep on my stomach.

One night, it was hot and the covers were down to my waist. I felt someone touch me, and whisper *good-night* in my ear. The next morning, I asked Mother if either she or Father had come into the bedroom before they went to bed. Had they touched me and said good-night? She gave me a funny look and said: "Of course not, and we're not going down that route again!" My heart sank with horror as I realized: *Oh no! They are touching me!* From that day on, I would sleep on my stomach with the covers pulled up to my head. My hands gripped the covers so tight that no one could pull them off.

Because no one understood me, I tried to push everything back and be as normal as everyone wanted me to be. But instead, I was made to feel that I was strange.

The day I started *Infants School*, my mother walked there with me.

On the way, I said: "Mother, do you know what my classroom is like?"

"Not unless it is the same one your sister was in, why?" she asked.

"Because I do," I said.

"Don't be stupid! You can't know, because you haven't been there before!"

"But I do," I said. "The room is blue and it has two pictures hanging on the wall, both of countryside views. The desks and chairs are in rows of six and the teacher is thin with long dark straight hair!" The words came rushing out of my mouth.

Mother bent down, looked me in the eye and said: "That's enough! Stop it and be quiet."

I did as I was told and thought: *I know I'm right! No one believes me!*

When we arrived at the school, we went through the big front doors. Mother asked where the First Year classroom was, and was told that it was down the corridor, the first room on the left. We walked into the classroom where the First Year teacher met us. Mother took a step back with surprise and her face turned white. The teacher and the classroom were just as I had described. The very tall teacher looked down at me and asked for my name. Before I could respond, Mother said: "It's Patricia." Then, she abruptly left.

My first day at school was difficult. I seemed to know where I was, yet, I felt like I was in a different time. My mind kept wandering and I could see the room visibly change as though it was a different time period with different children. I rubbed my eyes, because I couldn't believe what I was seeing. The teacher kept looking at me. We were given time to lie down and sleep in the afternoon, but I couldn't fall asleep. I kept seeing children walking around the room. They came, stood by me and talked to me. I was frightened but didn't dare say anything, because no one would believe me.

At the end of the day, my mother came to pick me up. She and the teacher walked over to the far side of the room where they had a quiet discussion about me. Even though I was not close by, I could hear every word they said. Mother explained that I was a little different and that the doctor said I would change when I started school.

We went home, and when Dad came in from work, we all had our tea together around the table.

During tea, Mother said: "We need to talk about Patricia."

"Ok," Father said.

After the dishes were washed, they both sat in the kitchen discussing me. I was playing with my brother and sister but could hear every word as though they were in the same room. They were talking about what had happened that day at school. Mother believed that there was something wrong with me. Father said that I was different, but that I was fine.

Chapter Four

Angelic Intervention

I was not a pretty girl at school. I was little and fat (with glasses) and my mother dressed us old-fashioned. Everyone thought we were poor. I was called names that were so cruel that sometimes I wondered whether it was worth being alive. My self-esteem was lower than a snake's belly.

People used to call me: *ugly, fat, old fashioned, weird, strange* and a lot more. I would often find a quiet place away from everyone and sob my heart out. It was pointless to talk to my mother, because she wouldn't have done anything. Most of the time, I felt alone. I wondered why I was alive and why I had to go through this on my own.

When I felt like this, I would get a vision of a *Being* that looked like an angel. He gave me his name as *Raphael*. He told me that my pathway would not be easy, but I would heal many people in my lifetime, and I would understand when I was older. He kept telling me I was very special. At this time, I didn't know much about angels, and wondered whether I was seeing things or going mad. If no one else could see what I could see, how could I believe it? How could I ever talk about it to anyone and who would believe me? Raphael always seemed to appear at the right time (when I needed someone to talk to) and he calmed me down. So, I accepted it as something that I needed at the time. I never talked to anyone about these visions until much later in life.

Chapter Five

Losing Bess, Finding Sight

My father loved dogs so we always seemed to have one dog after another. One pedigree dog that we had (Bess) was a golden retriever, and had a mean streak (according to my mother). I would play with her, climb on her back and go for a ride. I used to talk to her as a friend and she would look at me as though she knew what I was saying. No one would dare enter the gate if Bess was loose, because she would try to bite. With me, though, she was always loving and gentle, as though we had a connection. Sadly, my father had to have her put down. I cried my eyes out because I had lost my best friend. I shouted at my mother: "I blame you for hating Bess and me!" and ran out of the house.

I was only three at the time. I remember that I didn't want anyone to find me, so I found a perfect secret place that I could crawl into. I sat there watching through the hole to see if anyone had followed me. I cried and cried for what seemed like ages when I saw Bess running towards me, wagging her tail. My father was following close behind. She had brought my father to find me so I wouldn't wander off, get lost or be harmed. I couldn't believe my eyes. My father put his hand in the hole and said: "Come on, let's go home."

"How did you find me?" I asked.

"I don't know, really. I just felt I should come this way and my eyes were drawn to the hole, and there you were!" he said, looking puzzled.

"We'll get another Bess, don't worry. You can come with me to choose one," he said.

"But Bess isn't gone. I just saw her. She came to the hole and I stroked her!" I said.

"No, she's gone" he replied. "I saw it with my own eyes." He gave me a look that implied: *How could you have seen her?*

I went along quietly, because no one would believe what had happened.

When a couple of weeks had passed, my father said: "We are going to the dogs' home to find another dog, so get yourselves ready. We're leaving in half an hour."

We all piled into the car. It took us about 45 minutes to get there and when we walked in the front door we were met by a big woman with glasses. As she peered down at us, her glasses slid down to the end of her nose.

"So you want a new dog, do you?" she asked.

"Yes please," I replied, timidly.

The woman stood up and said: "OK, let's go and have

a look at some dogs and see what you think." She walked out of the main area and down a long corridor.

At the bottom of the corridor was another door and as we got nearer, we could hear dogs barking. The woman pushed the door open and there in front of us were hundreds of dogs. However, I could see more than the dogs. I could see different colours. In fact, I could see all the colours of the rainbow. I couldn't believe what I was seeing. I rubbed my eyes and looked again. The colours were even more vibrant.

My mother looked down at me with a puzzled expression, and said: "What's up with you?"

"Can you see all the colours?" I asked.

"There are no colours, so stop it!" she said with anger.

The woman gave me a knowing look and asked: "What colours?"

"Oh, there's nothing. She daydreams a lot!" my mother quickly said, as she grabbed my hand and pulled me away.

I could see stripes of colour around each dog and, as I touched them, the colours changed, like magic. I was so excited! I had never seen anything like it. It was just like walking into *Alice in Wonderland* - but no one would have believed me. At that moment, a white swirling light appeared, and suddenly, Bess came through the light wagging her tail and running around me.

"Stop fidgeting!" Mother said, shaking my hand. At that point, Bess jumped back through the white light and it all disappeared. I hated my mother for sending Bess away. I pulled away from her and ran off to play with one of the dogs. It snuggled into my lap, and while I was stroking it, the colours kept changing from yellow to pink and then to blue. I could feel heat in my hands and then they turned blue. I could see this blue colour pouring into the dog's body.

The woman came over and said: "This one can't leave. She's ill."

"You think she is going to die, don't you?" I asked. The woman looked puzzled.

"Well, she isn't going to die," I said. She'll be better in three weeks. You'll see."

At that point, my mother came rushing over and grabbed me from the floor. "Now stop that!" she said.

"That's all right," the woman said. She looked at me in a way that said she hoped I was right.

During this time, Father had been walking around the dogs trying his Polo trick. The dog that ate the Polo mint is the one that he would take home with him.

"I want this one," Father said, as he pointed to a black and tan, Heinz variety puppy.

The woman picked up the dog and said: "That's a good choice."

My mother put us all in the back seat of the car while Father sorted things out with the woman. Ten minutes later, he got into the car and handed over the new puppy to my brother in the back seat. She was a lively little thing, climbing all over us all and biting anything she could.

"What are we going to call her?" I asked.

"'*Bess*, of course," he replied. Father always called his dogs *Bess*, so that wasn't a surprise!

Divine Intervention

I kept thinking of all the colours that I had seen around the dogs and wondered what it meant. Everyone thought that I daydreamed all the time - if only they knew! I used to think everyone could see the same things I could, but the more I talked about the things I saw, the more I realized that they didn't.

Bess was growing up and I played with her a lot. The interesting thing was, every time I touched her, my hands would turn blue, and I could see different colours around her. I had no idea what it was and I couldn't talk to anyone about it because they would think I was mad or daydreaming.

Six weeks after we got Bess, there was a knock at the door. My mother opened it and there was the woman from the dogs' home.

"Come in," Mother said.

"I thought I'd pop around and see how the dog was doing," she said. My mother offered her a cup of tea and set the table. When we had visitors the good tablecloth always came out along with the best china.

"Well, the dog looks happy and in good condition," the woman said.

"Yes, her name's *Bess* and she's settled in very well," Father replied.

"By the way, do you remember the dog that was ill? She made a remarkable recovery in three weeks, just as your daughter said she would!"

Everyone became quiet, then my mother said: "Oh, that was just a coincidence," and changed the subject.

I hated my mother for putting me down and for not accepting that there was something different about me that was good. She always made me feel like a freak show that you never talked about.

The woman looked at me and smiled as if she knew something. She turned to my mother and said: "I will have to go. Thank you for your hospitality and don't be so hard on your daughter!" Then she left.

That comment created thunder and lightning in the house. My mother was furious!

"What have you said to that lady?" she shouted, pointing her finger at me.

"Nothing!" I said, as I ran upstairs crying. No one understood me or even wanted to try. I was just this freaky girl to everyone. It felt like no one cared.

The day passed and no one said a word to me. It was as though I did not exist, so I went for a walk in the fields. As I sat down, a rabbit suddenly appeared and sat beside me. Then, four butterflies and a cat joined us. The colours around them were so vivid. As I touched them, the colours kept changing. It became a game – what colour would be next? This was very real to me, and not a daydream.

My visions began to get stronger. I could see colours around animals, plants and foliage. I could also see faces in the bushes and trees. In fact, it grew so strong that faces would appear everywhere on: carpets, walls, doors, pathways, furniture, toys, books, the ceiling, and on anything that I could hold in my hands.

How could I tell anyone about this? No one would believe me. I felt so alone and isolated. Everything felt like a heavy burden. I didn't know how to deal with all these strange occurrences, so I would try to shut them off. I just wanted to be normal and have someone love me, but that was difficult because my mother couldn't show love, and Father tried to keep the peace as much as possible.

I tried so hard to push these things back - to be normal - because everyone, (including the kids at school) saw me as strange. I felt different from everyone else. I certainly didn't feel that I belonged here with my family, or even on this planet! I really did feel that I should be somewhere else. Nevertheless, this is where I was and I had to make the most of it.

Chapter Six

Animal Cruelty

W̶hen I was young, we would visit relatives who I really didn't like or get along with. This was a result of their response to me. They always showed more interest in my brother, Terry and my sister, Angela.

Once, we all went to see my Auntie Lily and Uncle Norman in Filey, North Yorkshire. They had a farm with chickens, cattle and Christmas turkeys. We visited around Christmas time, and as I wandered around the farm, I went into one large group of sheds, where all these chickens were squashed up in cages. I ran out, crying, because I wanted to let them all go free. In fact, my emotions were running high, so I went back in and started to undo the cages. The chickens looked so sad, and I could feel their pain and anguish. I just couldn't stand to feel their emotions. They could hardly move around, let alone eat. Uncle Norman came in (as I was opening the cages) and shouted for my mother to control me. No one could understand why I was doing this. Mother grabbed me by the arm and dragged me out of the shed, leaving Uncle Norman to clean up after me.

Mother screamed at me: "What do you think you are doing?"

"They were hurting and in pain! I couldn't let them live like that!" I cried.

"It's nothing to do with you. Now, go and play with your sister and your cousin Mary," she said with anger.

"I don't want to," I replied.

"You will do as you're told, now go over there to your sister!" she said.

I started to walk towards them and looked back to see if she was watching. She had walked off towards my father, so I quickly scurried around the corner of one barn and started to walk towards another. I was curious.

What's inside the barn? I thought. My curiosity got the better of me so I opened the barn door and walked in. I was horrified by what I saw. There in front of me were hundreds of turkeys, all hung up by their feet on what looked liked skewers. Blood ran down their necks and beaks, just dripping into buckets. I turned as white as a ghost and screamed out loud. Everyone came running in to see what had happened.

"Look, look!" I cried, in panic.

"At what?" Mother snapped.

"The turkeys!" I cried.

My mother grabbed me by the arm and dragged me out of the shed. "That's normal," she said. "They have to be eaten at Christmas."

Divine Intervention

"I don't want any turkey for Christmas!" I said, sobbing my heart out.

"You are more trouble than you're worth," she said as she dragged me into the farm kitchen. "Just sit there and don't move. I do *not* want to hear another word from you," she said, as she pushed me onto a kitchen chair. My heart was in my mouth, so I couldn't say anything. I just listened to everyone else.

Everyone was talking about what had happened and my mother was apologizing to my Aunt Lily and Uncle Norman. I heard her say: "She is always like this."

At that moment, my angel appeared in front of my mother. I felt I was somewhere else. "Don't worry, Patricia, no one understands you, that's all," she said, and then she disappeared.

Chapter Seven

Buttercups, Daisies and Raphael

*I*often felt like Cinderella, and that made me even more determined to be famous and successful, to show everybody who I was and what I could do.

I really didn't get along with my cousin Mary, because she was spoiled. Mary and my sister, Angela, would go off and play, leaving me out of things, so I would just wander around and do my own thing. I always wished that I was older, so I could do what I wanted and make my own decisions.

"Look at her. She is in a dream world again," I heard my mother say, as she pointed at me.

"No, I'm not," I said.

"Just you be quiet! I do *not* want to hear another word from you!" she snapped.

I was both angry and bored.

Divine Intervention

I heard my mother and Auntie Lily talk about my cousin, Mary, who was coming to stay at our house, and then Auntie Lily could return the favour. "I will have everyone but Patricia," my Aunt Lily said.

My mother paused and said: "I can't let two come, and leave one behind."

"Well, I can't cope with Patricia," Aunt Lily replied. "Terry and Angela can help their Uncle Norman around the farm, but we can't handle Patricia," she said firmly.

I felt like a piece of meat. Everyone always talked *about* me, but not *to* me. It was as though I didn't exist. People didn't care what they said in front of me. I could feel my emotions welling up, and suddenly, I jumped off the chair and shouted: "I am here! Can't you see me? Do I not have feelings? Or, is it that you all just don't care? You know, I hate you all!" I said, as I ran off to the fields, crying. I ran up to the top field and sat down, surrounded by buttercups and daisies, sobbing my heart out.

At that moment, a beam of white light appeared, and another angel was there, with beautiful colours of blue, green and gold. He was so tall, with big wings that opened out like the wings of an eagle. My heart began to pound with excitement.

"Who are you?" I stuttered.

"Raphael," he answered, in a smooth and calm voice that made me feel tingly all over. "Why are you so sad, Patricia?" he asked.

"No one likes me or cares for me. I feel so alone," I replied.

"Patricia, you are just different from everyone else. Your pathway is spiritual and you have to feel all of these emotions to grow. I know it can be painful, but we gain great strength from our own pain. Helping others to understand is your pathway, so you have to feel what others will feel to help them in the future. I will guide you through these times. You are not on your own," he said calmly. He looked at me with great compassion and then, he disappeared. Raphael looked so different this time but I did not question it.

I felt calm and relaxed. My tears had stopped, and I found myself almost floating as I walked back down the fields to the farmhouse.

As I arrived at the house, my mother came rushing towards me shouting: "Where have you been? You've been gone for over two hours and we want to go home."

"It doesn't feel like two hours. I've only been gone a short while," I replied.

"No, Patricia, you *have* been gone for over two hours." Father said. I've been looking for you and couldn't find you. Where have you been?"

"Just to the top field of buttercups and daisies. I sat for a while," I said.

"But, I went up there and looked for you, and there was no sign of you," Father said, looking puzzled.

"So, where have you been?"

"I was up in the top field, sitting with the buttercups and daisies!" I cried.

"Well, I don't know, I must have missed you in the mist then," Father said, as he opened the car door for me to get in.

But what mist? How could he have missed me? I could see all around me. The sun was shining. There was no mist and

Divine Intervention

I never saw my father! I thought. This was all I could think about on the way home. I stared out of the car window, watching the views change from countryside to towns to villages, until we got home.

As soon as we got in, my mother insisted that we all have a bath and go to bed, as it was late. I rushed upstairs, got my bath, jumped into bed and turned out the light. My mind was full of what had happened up in the field, so I couldn't sleep. I could hear everyone come upstairs to go to bed, and I kept my eyes closed so that they would think I was asleep. I felt Angela get into bed and heard my mother and father come into the bedroom. "She's asleep now, but I don't know what we're going to do with her," my mother said.

"She'll grow out of it and turn out all right," Father replied. Then, they both walked out of my room and into their own bedroom.

I couldn't sleep. I could only picture the field and the events that had taken place. The image of the angel was so clear. As I replayed it all in my mind, I could see only sunshine and a clear blue sky. No mist was there. *What could have happened?* I thought.

At that moment, a white light lit up the room and the Angel Raphael appeared again. "Don't be puzzled Patricia. You were the only person who was meant to see me. Your father did come to find you, but you were safe with me and disguised from your father. We needed to talk, and I needed to help you. You have a curious mind that works overtime, Patricia. Go to sleep now, and we will meet again to talk sometime soon," he said, and then disappeared.

Divine Intervention

I felt myself drifting to sleep thinking: *Am I talking to myself, or am I really seeing and talking to an Angel called Raphael? If so, why does he disappear before I can ask him anything?*

"Go to sleep Patricia, we will talk later" I heard Angel Raphael reply, and I fell into deep sleep.

The next morning, I woke up feeling good about myself. I had a wonderful dream, spending time in the clouds with the angelic beings, and visiting lots of places that I had never seen before, wishing I could return there. Everyone made me feel so special and it renewed my zest for life.

I got up, washed and came downstairs with a spring in my step, humming the song: *The Lords My Shepherd.*

"What happened to you during the night? You're in a better mood today," Mother asked.

"Nothing, I just feel good, that's all," I replied, sitting down at the breakfast table.

Chapter Eight

Raphael to the Rescue

Sunlight bounces off crystals and shimmers rainbows across my healing room. An older woman sits in front of me with great anticipation. I can feel her depression as I begin the reading. She had lost her husband about seven years earlier. We were just about to start.

The inside temperature started to rise and the crystals began to beam light all around the room with swirling pools of rainbow colour. One of my crystal mirrors began to light up and a pool of fog started to exit the centre of the mirror. A misty fog started to form and an angel appeared with all the colours of the rainbow. It was Raphael. He showed his colours of blue/green and filled one side of the room with his presence, colour and calmness.

Divine Intervention

At that instant, like a flash, I was out of my body looking down on myself. I could see and hear everything. I was talking to this woman, describing her husband in great detail and she began to cry. At that moment, Raphael turned and out of another mirror, a mist began to form. This time it formed into her husband's spirit, just as I had described him.

The room grew hotter and hotter. When I saw her husband put his arm around her, I asked if she could feel anything. "I have just gone hot and a great feeling of his love as come over me," she said as she burst into tears. Her husband gave her the answers she needed to be able to grieve fully and carry on. She was so lost without him and had even thought of committing suicide because she missed him so much.

Even though this woman was guided to me, her answers came from heaven. As Raphael and her husband disappeared, I found myself back in my body talking to her. She said: "I was not going to come because I have been to other mediums before and have received nothing, but something kept telling me I should come and I am so glad I did. I will never forget today and what it has done for me. I feel that you are such a special person."

"The message was sent from heaven above, not me", I said. "I am just the instrument to channel their words. It has truly been a special moment for both of us," I replied.

A couple of days later, I was going through one of my self-questioning modes: Where does it come from? Who is it? Then I realized: this is what my father taught me to do. He said: "Never get complacent. Always question things, and when you do, they will always amaze you."

I was certainly amazed and honoured to have experienced what I did in that healing. The whole room was filled with such light and love that it took my breath away. These are such special moments in our lives. I wished everyone could see and experience such love – love that they bring to us in our time of need. Then, we would all know what real love feels like. To have experienced it in my lifetime, makes make feel grateful, honoured and humbled, all at the same time.

Chapter Nine

Ousting Cousin Mary

Your cousin Mary is coming to stay for a week. She's arriving tomorrow. You will have to sleep three in your bed, so I want no trouble, do you hear?" mother said sharply, pointing and waving a spoon at me.

"Why do you always think it's me that causes trouble? Why can't it be Angela or Mary?" I replied. "Do you know, I can't even get up in the morning and feel good about myself, without you spoiling it for me. Why do you do that, Mother?" I asked, feeling my emotions well up inside.

"Don't talk rubbish, child!" she snapped. "If you don't hold your tongue, you won't go out to play!" she said with anger.

I jumped out of my chair, ran across the room and opened the door. Looking at my mother, I cried: "You can't stop me! I *am* going out to play and I am *not* coming back into this house! I hate you!" I ran off up to the fields, trying to hold back the tears. I found my own field of buttercups and daisies, sat down in the middle of it, and hoped that I would see my angel, but he never appeared.

I felt so unhappy. I couldn't understand why my mother hated me so much, and why she hated (even more) to see me happy. I didn't want my cousin, Mary, to share my bed with Angela and me. Then, there would be two against one. Angela would always make sure that she got me into trouble. *This next week is going to be a nightmare!* I thought. Cousin Mary was definitely spoiled and selfish. I couldn't stand her.

I sat in the field, looking at the clouds, seeing all sorts of faces and animals in the sky. *Why can't everyone else see what I can?* I wondered. I had always been able to pick up feelings about things, events and people, and I often wondered how I could do it. My feelings were always right, but how could I explain this to anyone without sounding like a know-it-all? I never really had any true friends because I was always different than everyone else, and they always seemed puzzled or frightened of me.

I suddenly looked at my watch and jumped up quickly. I had been out of the house for hours and Father would be home from work. I rushed down from the fields, not stopping for anyone or anything.

As I came around the corner to our street, I bumped into Angela. "You're in deep trouble. You wait and see," she said, with a smug look on her face.

"Oh, get lost, you're sick!" I replied. "You've always liked to see me in trouble, so go fly a kite!" I said, pushing her out of my way as I ran towards the house.

I stopped at the gate to catch my breath and my mother appeared, shouting: "Where have you been?"

"Just walking by myself," I replied cautiously.

"Get in this house *now!*" she screamed. I opened the gate and slowly walked down the path to the door. I knew what was coming, so I wasn't in a hurry to get there. As I got to the door, she grabbed me by the arm and hit me again and again. I suddenly found the strength to pull my arm free and ran for the stairs door. My mother came running after me. My heart was pounding.

I got to the top of the stairs, turned and looked at my mother. "You hit me again and I'll go to the police and tell them you batter your kids!" I shouted.

She stopped dead in her tracks and I ran off to the bedroom and locked the door.

Ten minutes later, I heard footsteps coming up the stairs. "Are you going to let me in?" Father said. I was crying as I walked to the door and opened it. "What have you been up to?" he asked.

"Nothing. Mother upset me this morning and I ran out of the house and went for a walk. I just lost track of time, that's all. But nothing is forgiven in this house. I just can't do anything right and I don't feel that I belong here!" I sobbed.

"Of course you belong here. Your mother just doesn't understand you or know what to do because you are so different from your brother and sister, that's all," he replied.

"No, she hates me! I know it! She's so different when you're not here. You don't see it and I can't keep going like this, I really can't!" I cried, blowing my nose and wiping the tears from my cheeks.

"Come on downstairs and have some tea. You have to eat," he said, holding his hand out and pulling me up off the bed. He put his arm around me and walked me down the stairs into the kitchen.

"Come on Mother, give the girl her tea," he said, looking at her.

"You sit down there and let's put an end to this," he said, pulling my chair out and indicating with his hand for me to sit down.

"That's the end of it now," he said, turning and looking at my mother. She never said a word. She placed my tea on the table without looking at or touching me and then walked off into the living room. The house was quiet. No one said a word while I had my tea.

Once I had finished, Father said: "It's late. You better get a bath and get into bed."

"Ok," I said, and left the kitchen to go upstairs. I knew what that meant: a big powwow about me. *What do I care? No one really cares about me, and Father is just trying to keep the peace as usual. Nothing ever changes.* I thought. I really wanted to see my angel again but he didn't come. I really wished I could be somewhere else. I bathed and went to bed to get some real sleep, as cousin Mary was arriving in the morning.

I woke up the next day and Mother was in a bad mood. She was not yet over the events of the previous day, and of course, Cousin Mary was arriving in two hours. *What fun,* I thought.

"Don't you go wandering off today, as I want you here

to meet your cousin Mary," she grumbled at me.

"Ok," I muttered. I knew it wasn't worth saying anymore. She was really in a bad temper.

I walked into the garden and decided to spend time sitting and watching the birds and butterflies. The two hours seemed to fly by. Suddenly, Mother shouted from the kitchen window: "Your cousin Mary is here, so come inside and meet her." I obeyed her call, as it was not worth the aggravation. I got up and walked to the house to see my Auntie Lily, Uncle Norman and Mary getting out of their car in the drive. What a performance! Auntie Lily should have been on the stage. She was always showing off in her posh clothes, nothing out of place, and a daughter who followed in her footsteps.

Auntie Lily and Uncle Norman stayed for about two hours. We had non-stop tea, food and a lot of nonsense conversation, with everyone trying to be polite and on their best behaviour. No one wanted to show any chinks in their armour. That's what I felt. The two hours were so false. Auntie Lily and Uncle Norman had to get back to the farm by daylight, and that for me, was such a relief. After they had said their goodbyes and left, my mother showed Mary where the bedroom was. She had made space for her clothes, so she could settle in. My sister, Angela, spent time with her unpacking and they were giggling and talking in the bedroom. I stayed downstairs. It was like having two three-year-old children, and I couldn't stand Mary.

The evening passed, and my mother eventually told us to go upstairs, get a bath and go to bed. We all went upstairs and then there was an argument about who was going first, brought on by Angela, who was showing off in front of Mary. I couldn't be bothered, so I let everyone else go first. When it was my turn, there was no hot water, and my mother came upstairs shouting at me for not being in bed. It was no use saying anything to her, as it would have only caused more trouble. I had a quick cold wash and got into bed.

Mary was sleeping between Angela and I. They kept talking and giggling so loudly that my mother came in, blamed me for the noise, and told me to go to sleep. Mary and Angela found it so funny. They couldn't stop laughing at the fact that I had gotten into trouble. I had enough, so I jumped up and threw myself across the pair of them and began hitting them both. They started screaming for my mother, who came running in shouting: "What's going on?"

"Pat keeps hitting me and Mary for nothing!" Angela said.

Mother grabbed me by the arm, pulled me out of bed and shouted: "You can sleep on the sofa tonight!" I looked over at Angela and there was a selfish smirk on her face.

"It wasn't me, it was those two!" I cried.

"I don't want to hear anymore about it. You're sleeping on the sofa and that's that!" she said with anger. I couldn't win, so I kept quiet. What was the point when my mother had made up her mind that it was my fault? I went down stairs and slept on the sofa. The only problem with sleeping downstairs was that my mother got up at 4:30 in the morning to light the fire, fix Father's breakfast and see him off to work.

Consequently, I had little sleep before my mother got up the next morning.

Divine Intervention

A week seemed like a life sentence to me. *Our Mary will be here for seven days!* I thought.

Things didn't get any better as Angela and Mary stuck together and made sure that I got into trouble. I was grounded for the whole week for fighting with them. I thought: *In for a penny, in for a pound.*

I knew that whatever I did, I was going to get into trouble, so I might as well do something to get into trouble rather than have them blame me for something I didn't do. After five days, I had had enough. I decided to scare them, so I found one of Mother's white sheets and cut holes in it for the eyes, nose, and mouth. I waited until everyone went to sleep and snuck out of bed, putting the white sheet over my head and letting it hang down my body. I started making ghostly noises, and pushed Angela and Mary to wake them up. This continued for about ten minutes, when Mary finally woke up, saw the ghostly figure and screamed her head off. This woke the whole house up. I quickly dropped the white sheet and pushed it under the bed. I jumped back into bed as though I was asleep.

Mother came rushing in to see what had happened. Mary described the ghostly figure and Mother came to the conclusion that she had had a bad dream. I felt better that I had gotten back at her, and my mother never related it to me. Now, I knew how to get even with Mary.

I bought rubber spiders with my pocket money and put them in the bed. When we went to sleep that night there were screams from Mary, and mother came running in. "There's a spider in the bed, Auntie Ada!" she cried.

My mother flung the bedclothes back and found the rubber spider. "Is this your doing, Patricia?" she asked.

Divine Intervention

"No mother, I've never seen it before" I replied, with a smug look on my face.

"Are you sure?" she snapped.

"Of course I'm sure," I lied. There was no proof, so she couldn't blame me, which she hated.

"I want to go home!" Mary said, crying.

"I will phone your mother in the morning, and see what she has to say," she replied.

The next day came and there was a conversation on the phone between Auntie Lily and Mary. It was all so pathetic. She was treated like a little doll, and guess what? My Auntie Lily came all the way from Filey to pick her up that day.

There were big discussions in the kitchen between my mother and Auntie Lily. Auntie Lily didn't like me and she was trying to blame me for Mary wanting to leave. My mother agreed with her. Father stepped in and said that it was enough talking about me, but there was no proof that I'd been involved. I loved my Father for that, as he was the only one who would stand up for me.

Auntie Lily stayed for about two hours and left with Mary in tow. That really pleased me. Now, I could get back to normal and not have a spoiled brat to contend with. There was total silence from my mother for about two days. She would have loved to blame me but she couldn't find positive proof that would incriminate me.

Chapter Ten

Hairdos from Hell

M y mother was very old-fashioned so that's how she dressed us. One day, she said: "I have booked an appointment for you both to go to *Mrs. Burkenshaw's Hairdressers* to have your hair cut and permed."

My sister and I looked at each other in horror. That's where all the old folks used to go. We used to call them *The Blue Rinse Brigade*. Both of us were trying to grow our hair long, so we were in a state of sheer panic.

"I don't want my hair cut and permed, I'm growing it!" I said.

"You will do as you are told. It'll be easier to manage and I won't hear another word spoken!" she snapped.

Not another word was said. It was pointless. She had her mind made up. We were already dressed in round-toed shoes, when everyone else wore pointed-toed shoes.

Most everyone wore stockings while we were in three-quarter-length white socks. This was a nightmare. This was the last straw!

The day came and Mother took us to Mrs. Burkenshaw's place to make sure we went through the door.

"I will leave the two of them with you. You know what I want, so don't let them tell you any thing different. I'll be back to pick them up later," she said, as she walked out the shop door.

"Who's going first?" Mrs. Burkenshaw asked.

"She is," my sister said quickly. I never got a chance to say anything because Mrs. Burkenshaw grabbed my arm and placed me in the chair. I closed my eyes, as I dared not look. I could hear the scissors cutting and then the horrible smell of the perm.

"You can sit there while I do your sister," Mrs. Burkenshaw said. I still couldn't look, but I heard my sister get into the next chair and the sound of the scissors started all over again.

The next three hours seemed like a lifetime. The end result was a straight bit of hair followed by a big ball of frizz. It was horrible! How could I go to school with this hairdo and not be the joke of the school? My mother came and picked us up, and we walked home, both of us crying all the way.

"You can stop crying. There is nothing wrong with your hair," she said with anger. When we got home we both ran upstairs sobbing. Neither of us went out of the house all weekend.

When Monday came, we had to go to school and

believe you me; we had much to contend with. Kids called us names and laughed in our faces. I just couldn't bear it any longer.

My friend Susan said: "Come to my house, we can try to iron it straight." We tried for an hour to straighten my hair. It helped a bit, calming down the frizz, but we couldn't straighten it properly.

My sister and I decided that drastic measures were needed, so I cut her hair and she cut mine. Our hair was in such a mess. When Mother came in from shopping she went mad.

She took us straight down to Mrs. Burkenshaw's shop, and asked: "What can be done with their hair?"

"I can cut and style it short," she said. So my mother agreed and she stayed until it was done. She never said a word to either of us all the way home.

When we got into the house she said: "You two can stay in for a month for what you have done – no television and no friends." We both went up to our bedroom and just laughed. It didn't matter how long she made us stay indoors. We had just got a new haircut and no frizzy perm.

Chapter Eleven

Busted Noses & Chimney Sweeps

The more my mother withheld her love, the more I became a rebel. If that's how it is going to be, I thought, then I can't ever be a normal child in my mother's eyes, so why try?

I didn't like it that way, but I didn't know what to do to change it. For most of my life, up to that point, I had been feeling alone and excluded from the family. I didn't look like any of them, and felt so different that I just didn't feel connected to them.

I often wondered what my life would be like when I was older. I desperately hoped that it would be better than it had been. My happy memories seemed to be like shooting stars, gone in seconds.

I wanted to grow up and move away from home, because then I would be away from my mother's influence.

Divine Intervention

I remember, when I was little, the chimney sweep had been cleaning all the chimneys in the street and had left piles of black soot everywhere. I had been playing, and my mother shouted for me to come inside, change clothes and get ready to go out. Keith, who was a boy on my street, came to our house and asked if I could go out to play.

My mother said: "She can, but don't go far because we are going out shortly."

We went out to play, started arguing and he pushed me over. I fell right into a deep pile of black soot. When I stood up, I was black all over. Keith ran home laughing and I had to go home to face my mother. She went crazy. She couldn't smack me because the soot would fly everywhere, but she threw me into the bath with great force and ran the bath around me.

"I told you not to get into trouble," she said. "Now, look what you've done!" She scrubbed me down with a scrubbing brush and soap.

The brush hurt me so much that I could feel it grating against my skin.

"Sit still! This is the only way to get the soot off!" she snapped. I couldn't wait for it to be over.

"Now get out and dry off," she said with anger as she walked out of the door.

I looked in the mirror and my skin was bright red. I could hardly let the towel touch me.

"You hurry up! Your clothes are on your bed, so get dressed. We're going out soon," she shouted from the bottom of the stairs.

I dabbed my skin gently because I was feeling a great

deal of pain. I held the towel against me and went to the bedroom to get dressed.

I have to be brave, I thought, or my mother would come and dress me and that would be even more painful.

"Focus, Patricia," a voice said. I looked around and saw no one. "Focus on a lovely meadow and a running stream while you get dressed," the voice said, calming me.

"Who are you?" I asked.

"'Who I am doesn't matter just now. It's you that matters," the voice answered.

I kept looking around the room but could see no one, just a bright light flickering and moving around the room.

"Come down stairs now, we're going out!" Mother shouted.

At that point, the flickering light disappeared and when I looked down at myself, I had fully dressed without feeling pain.

What a miracle! I thought, as I slowly walked downstairs into the living room.

"Look at her! She looks like a lobster!" Angela said to my brother, Terry. They both laughed.

"It serves her right for going in the soot!" Mother snapped.

When my dad came in from work there was a big discussion about what had happened that day. I heard him say: "Well Mother, she is only a child and likes to explore. There's nothing wrong with that."

"Why do you always take her side?" Mother snapped.

"I don't, but Patricia isn't the same as Angela or Terry, and she needs to be treated differently from them. She is an explorer, very creative and needs to express herself in different ways," he replied.

"I don't believe that!" Mother said as she walked off.

Father came into the kitchen where I was sitting and looked at me. "You look a sight," he said, as he walked over to me to give me a hug.

"I know, and it hurts!" I cried.

"I can see that," he said. There was a great feeling of warmth from my dad and I loved him so much.

"You have to try not to wind your mother up so much, because she just doesn't know how to handle you," he said with affection.

"But it was an accident! I was playing with Keith and he pushed me and I fell in the soot. Mother never asks me what's happened! She just jumps to her conclusions!" I cried.

"I know, but just try to avoid confrontations with her," he replied.

"Ok," I sobbed.

"Now dry your tears and go and watch television before your mother comes down," he said, walking me to the TV room.

Just at that point, Mother walked through the stairs door. "What's going on?" she snapped.

"I have just told her to go and watch television and that's that!" Dad said with anger.

Mother stormed off into the kitchen and started washing the pots, while banging things about.

About an hour later, she walked into the room and said

sternly: "You go, get a bath and get into bed, Patricia."

I remembered what Dad had said, and got up and went upstairs. Even though I was enjoying watching television, and it was far too early to go to bed, it just wasn't worth it.

I had a lukewarm bath because my skin was sore and wiping my skin dry was very painful.

"Are you in bed yet?" Mother shouted.

"Just getting into bed now," I replied.

"Turn the light out and go to sleep!" she said with anger in her voice.

I quickly ran into the bedroom, switched the light off, but just sat on the bed. My skin was so sore that I couldn't stand the covers on my skin. I thought: At least she'll think I'm in bed.

I sat in the bedroom feeling a great deal of pain, when little orbs of coloured lights came flying into the room, swirling around my head. I could see blue, green, yellow, purple, orange and white. They made patterns in the air and went darting off around the room. I couldn't take my eyes off them. They made me smile. I wanted to laugh, but knew that Mother would hear me. I didn't want that to happen, because I would be in even more trouble. I kept my hand over my mouth so that I wouldn't make any noise. I watched the orbs play for what seemed like ages, and felt good about myself.

Suddenly, the stairs door opened and I heard my sister, Angela, say: "I am off to bed." The orbs disappeared and I quickly got under the bedclothes. I kept very still, as if I was asleep. I thought about the orbs, what or who, they were. I felt myself slowly drifting to sleep as I watched the orbs in my mind, spinning around the room.

I got up the next morning feeling a great calmness and looked in the mirror. My skin was red raw, but a lot of the pain had gone. How did the pain go so quickly? I wondered. I searched for an answer but couldn't find an explanation. I got dressed, went downstairs to the kitchen and sat. The cereal was in a dish in front of me, so I poured on the milk and just enjoyed it.

There was complete silence at the breakfast table, which felt uncomfortable, so I quickly finished my breakfast, picked up my things for school and left the house.

Mother never gave us time off from school. Her attitude was: you went to school and if the teachers sent you home, you were ill. So, I had to go no matter what. I was not looking forward to this, because I could not hide my skin.

I walked the long route to school, avoiding where other kids would walk and, as I arrived at the gate, everyone began to look at me. I tried to hide my face and look down at the floor so as not to make eye contact with anyone, but I could feel everyone looking and pointing. I could hear them talking about me. Even the teachers were looking but not asking questions. I felt I had the plague or something, because everyone was avoiding me.

About midday of my first day, kids started calling me names and that was the most hurtful thing of all. How can I say anything? I thought. It wouldn't make any difference. I hated being at school, but I couldn't go home. I felt on my own.

It took about six weeks for my skin to get back to

normal, and in that time, I took a great deal of criticism because everyone thought I had a skin disorder. How could I explain what had happened? No one would believe me. I knew I was on my own because even my so-called friends had deserted me.

My mother used to remind me of this incident as a warning of what could happen if I misbehaved. I used to try and side step her, so I wouldn't get into trouble (at least not as much trouble as I would have gotten into, if I had not learned to duck and dive).

I just wanted someone to like me and love me, but that did not seem to happen. Even my school friends thought I was strange. I never fit in and was never dressed in modern attire. In a sense, my confidence and self-esteem were low, but at the same time, that was also my driving force. It made me more determined to show everyone that I was somebody.

Chapter Twelve

Hospital, Eye Glasses & Faces

*I*couldn't figure out why people didn't understand me. I thought that Mother preferred my brother and sister to me. My sister, Angela, was her favourite. So, I used to play and fight with her because that was the only way I could get attention. As far as Mother was concerned, it was always my fault. Therefore, I went out of my way to prove her right. I became a problem child – always playing up. Nobody would listen to me so I would do things to get attention. One time, when the banister rail had just been painted, I carved my sister's initials into it to get her into trouble.

When I was five, I was absent from school, because I had chicken pox and measles at the same time. I was left with a lazy eye for which the doctor ordered surgery. I went into the children's hospital in Sheffield for the operation and woke up with bandages on my head. I didn't like the ward sister. She would try to force-feed me the hospital food, so I spat it in her face. After Mother argued with her about it, the woman left me alone. While I had on my bandages, I could sense things moving around the room and I knew that these were not living people. They would come close and whisper in my ear, telling me I would be fine. Once my bandages were off, I could see them walking around at night. They came and sat on my bed and talked to me. The ward sister told me it wasn't right to talk to myself. When I told her that I wasn't talking to myself, she gave me a strange look and muttered under her breath.

I sat on the hospital bed looking out of the windows and I could see faces in the clouds. At that time, I felt like I was from a different place and didn't belong in this world. I felt like it was my fantasy world - somewhere where I felt happy and no one could hurt me.

When I came out of hospital, I learned that I had to wear glasses to strengthen my eye and keep it out of the corner. I didn't want to wear glasses because my brother and sister didn't have to, and I felt, yet again, that I was the odd one out - that I didn't fit in. In fact, Father used to say that I was the *milkman's choice* because I didn't look like anyone else in the family.

Chapter Thirteen

Premonitions

*A*fter my operation, I went back to school where other things started to happen. I would see someone as they were, and then, I would see the same person again with a broken leg. This frightened me. In fact, within a few days, that person would have a broken leg, so I began to think that I could only see bad things. I didn't know what was happening to me. I began to think I wasn't normal, that I brought bad things to people because of what I saw. The kids at school used to think I was freaky and didn't have a great deal to do with me. I remember feeling so alone because I had no one to talk to. Kids can be so cruel when you are different. My fantasy world in the clouds kept me going and when I was there, I didn't feel so alone.

Divine Intervention

My school days were difficult but so was my home life. I felt close to my father and loved him so much but always had to fight for his attention. We would play practical jokes on each other. He would chase me around the garage and I would laugh. He was a calming influence in my life and I couldn't wait to get home from school and play games with him. I used to buy him drawing books for his birthday so he would sit down and draw with me. I loved to draw and he would help me. He also played the piano and I loved to sing along.

One night, when I was seven years old, I was drawing with my father and had a funny feeling. I asked him to stay at home with me the next day.

He laughed and said: "I can't do that, because I have to earn money to feed us all."

I wanted so much for him to stay at home with me. My mother came in at that point and told me to go upstairs, get a bath and get into bed, which I did. I couldn't sleep that night and felt really bad, as though something was about to happen, but I didn't know what. For the first time I didn't get a vision, just a feeling.

The next morning, I went down for breakfast. I asked Mother if Father had left for work and asked if he was ok. She gave me a funny look and said: "Of course he's all right!"

All day at school, I felt strange. I constantly thought about Father and felt sick, but still, there was no vision. At the end of school, I ran all the way home and into the house – where there were uncles, aunties and the doctor. As I peeped around the corner, there was Father just sitting, staring into space with a bandage around his leg. My heart sank and I shouted: "Dad!"

My uncle turned, pushed me out of the room and told me to stay in the kitchen with my brother and sister. He closed the door. I looked at them and felt that they thought it was my fault, so I sat quietly and listened. I could hear every word in the other room, even with the door closed. I heard that Father had had an accident down at the pit. The cutters had nearly sliced him up but he had managed to roll out of the way. They had cut a big hole in his leg. He also had a nervous breakdown while in the pit and that's why he just sat, staring into space. The doctor prescribed tablets and said: "Lets see how it goes," and then, he left.

We all felt lost. I could play with my dad one day and the next day he didn't even know me – he just sat, stared, and said nothing. I was angry – I wanted my father back! I ran up to my bedroom and asked my other worldly friends: "Why did you not show me? Why couldn't I stop it? Why did this have to happen to my father?"

When they came in from the spirit world, I shouted at them and told them to go away. I hated them and never wanted to see them again. I just wanted my father back.

Chapter Fourteen

Hard Times

*F*or the next couple of years, times were hard. My father couldn't work. He was in and out of the hospital and my mother had to keep the five of us on Social Security. They had to let the car go as it was on finance. They also negotiated a smaller payment on the furniture that they were paying for. We had to have school meals and the school policeman got us clothes, shoes and free milk. When the school policeman came to your house everyone knew that you were poor, and at school, your name was called out of the school register for not paying for your meals. At this time, I questioned everything. If I could see things and get visions, why would my spirit friends allow this to happen?

Father had stays in the hospital where he received shock treatments. Uncle Ted used to drive Mother and us to the Sheffield Hospital to see Father because Mother couldn't drive. We weren't allowed in to see him so we had to wait in the car. I used to look up at these tall ugly buildings and think: *What a terrible place for my father to be in.*

I kept asking, "When can I have my father back?"

By the time I was nine, Father was back at home and slowly getting better. The doctor said he could go back to work. He really didn't want to go back down to the pit, but the doctor said it would be fine and released him to return to work.

The Sunday before Father went back to work, I could feel the tension. Something was wrong because everyone was silent. Monday morning came. I got up and had breakfast but no one said anything. All day long, I had a funny feeling and couldn't wait to get home from school. I ran all the way home, but stopped at the back door with a terrible feeling in my stomach. I opened the door, slowly walked into the kitchen and looked through the crack in the door into the living room. There was Father sitting and staring into space. Mother was talking to the doctor. I heard the doctor say that Father had gone down into the pit shaft that day and experienced another nervous breakdown when he reached the bottom. They had to bring him straight back up to the surface. I thought it was all because of me. I didn't want to have these thoughts and feelings ever again, because when I did, Father would become ill. I was terrified of all the things I had experienced. I thought it was a bad omen for everybody. I ran outside around the back of the garage and sobbed my heart out. I felt so alone, and so afraid, like I didn't belong. *Why me?* I thought. *Why do I do this to people?*

Chapter Fifteen

Finally Understood

I prepared my healing room this particular morning as rainbow light poured in and shimmered above Titania (Queen of the Fairies) and my Angels. I watched the shimmers of light twist, turn and light Titania and my Angels as though they were on a stage. As I watched with amazement, the doorbell rang. I opened the door to greet a husband and wife I was not expecting. Someone had recommended me. They were having problems with their seven-year-old daughter. She was rebellious, showed no discipline and caused problems with the family. She kept missing school. Social services got involved and gave them a hard time. They were threatening to take their daughter into care if things did not improve.

The parents were desperate to find out what could be done. They had tried everything including counseling and psychiatric help but nobody could determine the problem.

I told them that I would like to see her with them but asked that they sit and say nothing while I worked with her. The appointment was made on the weekend so the husband could come.

On the first day, when I opened the door, I said hello to the parents, and there was this thin, little girl with long, blond hair. She looked down at the floor, twitched about on her feet and made it very clear that she really did not want to be here. "Hello," I said. "Please come in." We all walked into my workroom and her mother physically pulled her in and pushed her down onto a chair. Her eyes never looked at me but wandered around the room at my crystals. She lit up as she looked at every piece I had. I sat the parents in a far corner and placed a drawing pad and coloured pencils in front of the girl. Then, I sat and said nothing.

Her eyes gradually drifted to the paper and pencils and I just sat there and said nothing. Her parents were fidgeting in the background and a feeling of 'what is she doing' came to mind."

Because I was not asking anything of the young girl but just sitting, I could feel her sense of insecurity and what's all this about? But, I still did not say or do anything. After about half an hour, the girl started to draw of her own accord and I just sat and watched. The drawing was very interesting: her family and her house were at the bottom of the picture and there were figures floating in the sky.

"That's a nice picture. I like the figures in the sky,"

I said. The girl smiled. "Are these friends of yours?" I enquired. The girl smiled again, this time nodding her head.

"Will you draw me your favourite friend?" I asked. The girl did not hesitate and started drawing very quickly. In five minutes the picture was done. "What is his name?" I enquired. "George," she replied. There was a gasp from the back of the room. "Who's George?" I enquired. "My granddad and I do see him," she quickly said. "I know you do - so do I," I replied. Her granddad had been standing behind her and she had drawn his picture exactly as I had seen him.

"Her granddad is dead," the mother said. "I know," I replied. "But, that does not mean we can't see him." The little girl ran and sat on my knee and gave me a big hug. Her feelings of frustration and emotion welled up inside and tears of joy and relief came tumbling out.

"I am pleased to tell you that there is nothing wrong with your daughter. She is a very special child, that's all. We fear what we don't understand; therefore, we think that there has to be something wrong. A doctor would not understand that your daughter can see things that you or he cannot see, so she has become rebellious for protection and to get attention," I said.

"I would like to work with you and your daughter. You can learn what I do and see what gifts she has, so you can understand and help her," I said.

They happily agreed, as they had never seen their daughter take to anyone before, let alone do things without question.

We agreed to a session (once per week) and the

little girl jumped for joy. The next time they came, the child was first inside the door and headed straight for her chair, ready to do something with a big smile on her face. The father said: "I cannot believe the change in her this week. She kept asking: "When can we go back to see Patricia? Will she see me before Saturday? She has never been like this. I want to thank you for giving us our child back. You don't know what it feels like. I have never been into any of this and was skeptical about coming, however, I'm amazed at what you have done in one session, and whatever it takes from all of us, I want to learn and understand my daughter so I can help her."

I worked with them for over a year and, gradually, they learned what to do. They would sit down with her; ask what was happening, ask what she would see and show interest in her. Her school results improved, social services backed off, and she developed a better relationship with her family and others. Her brothers now tease her nicely because they also understand her.

That little girl is now eleven years of age and amazingly, she is into crystals, colours, sound and all forms of spiritual things. Her parents buy her books to read and she is astounding everyone. They all keep in touch. I am like her godmother. We banter by email and telephone and she still asks a lot of questions.

Chapter Sixteen

Like Father, Like Daughter

The next couple of years, the family went through the same things as before: no money, more hospital visits, more bills, and living off Social Security.

Father began to feel a little better. He was taking tablets for his mental illness when Uncle Thomas came around. He told Father that he went to a Spiritualist church, and asked: "why didn't he come?" After all, getting out could make him feel better. Father agreed to try it. Sunday arrived and both of my parents went to the Spiritualist Sunday service.

When they came home, Father looked a bit brighter. They both said they had enjoyed the service and would go again. Over a period of two months, they joined the *Open Circle at the Spiritualist Church* and Father learned that he was gifted as a Medium. From that point, he went on to learn spiritual healing, and toured the local churches. One Sunday afternoon, he threw his medication into the open fire and said that he would never need it again. Mother was horrified, but it was too late. The tablets were destroyed. He never took a tablet for his mind ever again.

Family life became more normal. Father found work in the Coal Board workshops and Mother got a part-time job.

I continued to see things and that still bothered me. One time, as I started down the stairs, I looked over my right shoulder to see the door open and black figures walk out of the bedroom. I wanted to scream but couldn't make a sound. I ran down the stairs, pushed the door open, slammed it shut and leaned back, catching my breath. Everyone was watching television.

"What's up with you?" Mother said. "You look like you've seen a ghost!"

"You wouldn't believe me if I told you," I replied and sat down. I became frightened and would never be in the house or in the dark alone if I could help it.

Even though I was scared of things, I would always joke about it with Father. When my parents went to church, I would ask: "Are you going to see the spooks again, Dad?"

He would laugh and say: "Very funny."

One evening, my parents went to church and my brother and sister were out. I loved to play the piano and sing, and my father's piano was so special to me. While they were gone, I played music and sang. Suddenly, I started singing: *The Lord's My Shepherd*. The door flung open and a strong wind blew through the room. I was horrified and for a moment (although it seemed like a lifetime), I couldn't move a muscle. It was as though someone had grabbed me so tightly that I couldn't breathe. Someone or something was crushing me. Then, finally, whatever it was, released me. I ran outside and sat on the doorstep until my parents came home. They arrived about 8:30 pm to find me in tears on the doorstep.

"What on earth is the matter?" Father said, as he hurried towards me. I explained my story.

"What were you singing at the time?" he asked.

"*The Lord's My Shepherd,*" I replied.

"That was your grandmother's favourite song! She wouldn't hurt you. You should have said Hello," he said.

"I didn't wait to find out," I said. My father gave me a cuddle, put his arm around me, and walked me into the house.

"Let's see if she's still here," he said. We went inside and everything was calm but the stairs door was still open. "She's gone," he said, as he walked over and shut the door. Although, I had come to terms with what I could see, I was still very frightened by it.

Even though Father's health was improving and he had found his new gift, it would be some time before he would learn about my unusual experiences and be able to help me.

PART TWO

Chapter Seventeen

Thoughts of Suicide

*I*once asked my father if he thought I was ugly. He smiled and said: "No, you're just growing up." You aren't fully grown yet. Remember the story of the ugly duckling waking up one day and seeing himself as a beautiful swan? That's what you'll be like. You just have to wait until it's your time. Why do you ask?"

"Oh, no reason," I replied. Many times, I thought of the ugly duckling and the swan, and those images helped me through my school years.

Outside my home, it was a different story. I was nobody's fool and would fight for my life, not caring what happened to me. I could stand up for myself very well and always made sure that teachers or parents never saw me fighting. It was a common occurrence for me to come home from school with torn garments, broken glasses and blood on my clothes. My mother used to get mad at me, because she would have to get me new clothes and another pair of National Health glasses. That was all she could think about. She never asked me why I'd been fighting. She didn't seem to care. I had many, many fights, and then the kids at school, one by one, finally left me alone.

As soon as I got in from school, my mother would scream at the top of her voice: "Look at you! You've been fighting again! Just look at your clothes! Get upstairs and no tea for you! Just get in the bath and go to bed! You can stay inside for the next couple of days!" I would run upstairs crying and go to my bedroom, feeling angry that no one cared about what was happening to me.

I found a way to get out of my bedroom, climb down the drainpipes, sneak out and sit at my favourite spot by the tree near the stream. I would sit there for (what seemed like) hours before going back home, and then, I'd get back into the bedroom the same way I got out. My parents didn't know for a long time that I escaped when they locked me in the bedroom, but my sister found me missing one day and told them. I didn't know that I had been discovered. The next time they locked me in the bedroom, Father was waiting just around the corner in the front of the house. He waited for me to climb down the drainpipe. I ran for my life and jumped over the wall. Father rarely hit me but I wasn't about to hang around and find out, just in case. I ran and ran until I came to my special place. Instead of sitting on the ground near the stream, I climbed the tree, and decided to stay put so no one could find me.

I knew I was going to get into trouble, so I thought about running away from home. No one loved me anyway. I was fourteen years old at the time. I couldn't be bothered with trying to fit in when I didn't stand a chance. I cried and cried at how useless my life was. Nobody could understand me, what was happening or how I felt.

I'd been in this space so many times, and here I was again. I didn't care if I had another vision or not. I just wanted to push everything away. I would have given anything just to be normal! I decided that I'd had enough, so I climbed to the top of this tall tree, determined to end it all. When I got to the top, the branch gave way and I fell. When I hit the ground, it was soft sludge and I was covered in it.

Raphael appeared again and said: "It is not your time to go."

"How would you know?" I screamed.

At that moment, he disappeared and I saw my father standing there.

"Who were you talking to?" he asked.

"Oh, no one!" I cried.

"Come on, let's go home and get you cleaned up," he said, holding out his hand.

Not another word was spoken as we walked home. Father opened the back door and we walked in. Then he told me to go and get a bath.

Mother was about to speak but Father looked at her and said: "That's enough for today, let it lie."

I could see that she was furious, but she said nothing as I left the room to go upstairs. I got a bath and went to bed, wondering why Father hadn't done anything.

Chapter Eighteen

Unexpected Visitors

*T*hat night I found it difficult to fall asleep, because I could see lots of faces on my bedroom wall. They would get bigger and come closer and closer to my bed. I was frightened, but could not move or make a sound. It was as though I was asleep, but not asleep. I felt myself being lifted from my bed, even though I couldn't move a muscle. A beam of light appeared and my body passed through it.

There were many beings in this mist and light. They were not anything like us, though. They had strange faces and bodies. They came around my floating body and looked me over. They didn't move their mouths but I could hear them talking to me.

"Don't be afraid," one said.

"You can talk to us through your mind and thoughts," said another.

"Who are you?" I asked.

"We are *Atlanteans*," one said.

"Who?"

"*Atlanteans*" another said.

"I've never heard of you."

"But you will when you get older," one replied.

"I want to go home."

"Then you will!"

My mother was pushing my shoulders, saying: "Come on! Get up, or you'll be late for school!"

I slowly got up and tried to determine what had happened. Had I been dreaming? I decided that I must have been because I had never heard of the *Atlanteans*, but it was all so clear and vivid. My mind questioned this for weeks. Who could I ask about this? No one.

Over the next few weeks, my dreams began to get brighter, more vivid and much clearer. These beings came into my dreams and told me that they were there to teach me. I thought I was going crazy. I'd talk to myself and thoughts would appear from nowhere to give me an answer. I got headaches; I heard noises and everything seemed to be much louder.

I can't take this much longer! I thought. I told my mother that I wasn't feeling well. She took me to the doctor who gave me tablets to relax the headaches. She also made an appointment for me to go to the hospital to have my ears checked. They couldn't find anything wrong.

My mother was mad. "You've made all this up and wasted everyone's time," she said.

"No I haven't!" I cried." I still hear noises and have

headaches. Why won't you believe me?" I sobbed, as I ran up to my bedroom.

The noises in my ears and the headaches continued for about six months. The pain in my head felt like someone was constantly drilling into my skull. I wasn't sure how much more I could take. Then one night, in my bedroom, when I was half asleep, I had another vision of an Atlantean, who said: "Just two more days and the pain and noises will stop. You're just having difficulty with our frequency and energy. All will be well, you will see." Then he disappeared.

I couldn't figure out what was happening and kept thinking that I must be crazy. However, after two days, just as predicted, the headaches and noises stopped. So how could I explain this? I felt different too. I could read people's thoughts more easily and my ears were so sensitive it seemed like I could hear a pin drop a half-mile away.

How could this be, I wondered, and immediately I got my answer: "You are one of us." Those words freaked me out. Who was the voice inside my head? How could I argue with myself? It was difficult, because I couldn't see who was talking to me.

Besides that, the sky looked bluer, the trees seemed greener, and everything looked more vibrant. In this vibrancy, I could see a brilliant haze around everything with lots of colours. It was glowing. Everything fascinated me. I had never seen things quite like this before.

I would be sitting in class, and yet I would see myself sitting in class. There seemed to be two of me, but only one of us was moving and the other could walk through walls! The first time it happened, I jumped out of my skin. The teacher looked at me and asked: "Are you all right, Patricia?"

"Yes, Miss Robinson," I replied.

When the lesson finished, she called me over. "Are you sure you're all right? You're as white as a ghost!"

"Yes, Miss. I thought I was going to faint and I felt a bit funny for a couple of minutes, but I'm fine now."

"Well, if it comes back, go and see the school nurse."

"I will Miss, thank you," I replied, and left the classroom.

Miss Robinson was very strict and had little tolerance for the unexpected. She seemed to know when people were faking it, so for her to notice something, and then hold me back after class and show concern was unusual. This confirmed to me that what I thought had happened, must have really happened.

What is all this? I asked myself.

You're learning our ways, someone answered in my head.

This is really freaky, I thought.

You will see as time goes on.

I tried not to think because every time I did, something or someone answered me. This made me fearful that I really was going mad. I was dreaming more; going to different places (some underwater), seeing unusual 'Beings', seeing lots of colours and experiencing things I'd never seen before. I saw a special room with lots of skulls that you could see through. The energy there felt so strong.

What's this all about? I thought.

You are being given the knowledge," someone said.

Divine Intervention

What knowledge? I wondered.

Atlantis.

But I don't know Atlantis, I thought.

But you will, someone replied.

I tried not to think at all, because I started to believe that I was really going mad.

At school, my artwork took on an unusual theme: I drew structures I'd never seen before, some above water and some below. The art teacher thought they were creative and futuristic. When I drew anything, it was as though I had a map or diagram in my head that I could see so clearly that I could sketch every detail. All these voices and pictures were in my head! I couldn't tell my mother, because she would reluctantly take me to the doctor and I would be declared insane. My anxiety grew about what was happening. Father kept looking at me. One day he said: "I think we'll let the doctor have a look at you. We'll go and see him tonight."

"Ok," I replied. We went to see the doctor and he checked me out, blaming my condition on puberty. *What a load of toss!* I thought.

After about twelve months, things began to settle down, as though everyone had disappeared. Then, one night, a 'being' appeared in my dream. He said: "You have what you need for the future, so you won't see us again." Then he vanished. I never saw them again and my life seemed to return to normal. I was so wrong.

Chapter Nineteen

Predictions and Dreams

*H*ave you ever sat in class and know what was going to be said, and by whom, before it was said? I have. I would write my notes and be so far ahead of everyone that my classmates would copy what I'd written. We were called into a meeting with Mr. Dollan, our teacher, and he informed us that our homework was identical. Therefore four out of five of us were cheating.

He said: "I'm splitting you all up, and we'll see what happens."

Unfortunately, my classmates were disciplined for cheating. I knew exactly what was going to be written on the blackboard before it was written. My homework was done in minutes rather than hours, however my sister would take all night.

Divine Intervention

Mother said: "You haven't done your homework, you're lying. So you can stay in until your sister has finished hers."

How could this be? Homework was easier for me, so why should I be penalized for being quicker than my sister? Things just seemed to be so unfair.

My mother thought a great deal about my brother who was the firstborn. I used to call him the *blue-eyed* boy. My sister was born next, and Mother saw her as being fragile and sensitive. Consequently, she spent a lot of time looking after her and making sure that she was ok.

Mother never really showed me any attention. The only thing I got was: "Your sister is going out, so you go with her and make sure she doesn't get into trouble!" There was no use in arguing with her, because she would make me stay in, if I refused. I hated going out with my sister because she would always aggravate people, and I would have to step in. I would end up fighting and would get into trouble for breaking my glasses and ruining my clothes. I tried telling Mother that it was Angela's fault, but she never believed me. I finally decided that if I was going to get into trouble anyway, I might as well make sure that I hit Angela first so she could feel my pain. I always ended up fighting with her, and she would call Mother, so I just made sure that I hit her hard before she could shout for her.

During this time, I began to dream at night - dreams that were so vivid and colourful. I kept seeing a lot of mist with rainbows shining inside. Over a two-week period, my dreams grew brighter. In one dream, a beautiful door appeared and began to open. I stared at the door because there was a beautiful calming light glowing through the cracks in it. My curiosity got the better of me so I took a deep breath and walked to the door, opening it fully.

I wonder what is through this door, I thought, and a voice answered me: *Walk inside. Don't be afraid.*

Suddenly, the white mist became a beautiful swirling pool of colour that gave me the feeling that I'd been here before. A great sense of peace and wisdom came over me. I could see faces in this pool of colour.

Who are you? I enquired.

We are Lemurians, one said.

I have never heard of you, I answered.

You know us from the past, a male voice said.

Come and sit with us, another said.

I cautiously walked through the door and sat down in the swirling pool of mist. I felt more confused than frightened. These faces didn't look human and they were speaking to me telepathically. There was a strong sense of calm and knowing.

Our link is strong with you, as you were once one of us, one said. My mind was racing.

How could I have been an Atlantean and a Lemurian at the same time? I thought.

Different life times, another said.

This is crazy! I thought, and suddenly, I woke up.

My mind contemplated this experience for weeks. During this time, I felt strange and my headaches reappeared. My ears were hearing funny noises and voices.

I can't take all this again! I thought.

You don't have too we are nearly done, a voice said.

Done with what? I thought, in panic.

Attuned you to our frequency, someone said.

I was not so frightened this time, because I had experienced these things before. The headaches, the noises and voices in my ears lasted another week and then disappeared.

My dreams over the next month were incredible. I questioned if they were real or a product of my imagination. I went to Merlin's Cave and spent time talking with him. I travelled to other planets and met other 'Beings.' I went to places where I saw many clear and coloured shapes (which I now know to be crystals). These places all seemed to be familiar to me, but I couldn't explain why. My head was like a computer ready to burn out, as there was all this knowledge working through my dreams. But, who could I tell? Nobody would believe me. I could hear my mother's words: "She's in her fantasy world again."

Then suddenly, just as my dreams appeared, they disappeared. I kept thinking what and where did this come from, and what did it really mean? I never got the answer to this until later in life.

About two months later, I started menstruating and for a while, nothing unusual seemed to happen. I thought that everything had changed and that I'd become normal again. No visions, no voices, no thoughts in my head, no smelling things that I couldn't see, no gut feelings and no dreams. I couldn't believe it! For once, I felt normal, so I concentrated on my schoolwork and my singing.

My mother really did not give us any sex education. She was very straight-laced and we didn't talk about 'sex'. If something came on the television, (like a man and woman sitting up in bed) she would change the channel. So the only preparation that I had for what was to come was learned from my school friends, and I had no way of knowing whether what they told me was true.

When I started menstruating, Mother asked: "What do you know about your periods?"

"Just what I've been told by my school friends," I replied.

"What's that?" she enquired impatiently. I explained what I had been told, and she said, "That's about right," and that was that. Preparing me for my life as a woman never seemed to enter her head.

Chapter Twenty

Innocent Deception

*E*ven though I had unusual visions and experiences, all I ever wanted to do was sing. Mr. Spinks (who was well known in the area) had many students who did well. He worked with choirs that performed in competitions and they used to win most of the time. People had a great deal of respect for him.

When I first went to Mr. Spinks, it was for piano lessons. Father couldn't read music, so he learned by listening to a piece of music, and then he would play it. He always wanted one of us to play the piano. My brother and sister didn't want to learn; therefore, I was nominated by Father and didn't really have a choice. A young man was taking singing lessons just before my piano lesson, and after about a year, I noticed a change in him. I used to love to hear him sing and would go early just to listen to him. Mr. Spinks could see that I was interested and asked:

"Do you want me to test out your voice?"

"Oh yes, please!" I said with excitement. I sang scales and a little song, and then he turned and looked at me. My heart was racing, because I was scared of what he might say.

"You have a beautiful voice. One that I would be pleased to train," he said.

"Really?" I asked with disbelief.

"You sound like you don't believe it," he replied.

"Oh no, it's just that I never thought my voice would be good enough!" I said.

"Your voice is lovely, we just need to work on it," he said.

"I don't think my parents can afford to let me do both piano and singing," I said.

"Then ask if you can change to singing lessons," he replied.

"Ok, I will!" I said as I packed up my music and left.

All the way home, I kept thinking how I might convince my parents to let me change from piano to singing lessons. My heart sank, because I knew that Father wanted me to play piano. As I arrived home, I opened the door and was met by my mother.

"What's the matter with you?" she asked. "You look like you've lost a five pound note!"

"Oh, nothing" I muttered. I knew that there was no way I was going to mention this to my mother. The right time never seemed to appear, however, because I couldn't seem to talk to my father by himself. There was always my mother, brother, or sister around. I just couldn't find the right moment.

Divine Intervention

Every day, I practiced my musical scales, while I played on Father's piano. Still not finding the right moment, I was convinced that he would never allow me to change.

My next lesson came and I wondered what I would tell Mr. Spinks. I walked up the path to his house and rang the doorbell. When he let me in, we walked into the music room and he said: "Well, what did your parents say?"

"They can't afford for me to do both, but it's all right to change to singing lessons, if I want to," I quickly said, not looking him in the eye.

"And what do you want to do?" he asked.

"I want to sing!" I replied.

"Then sing you shall!"

Mr. Spinks sat at the piano, and this time he started playing musical scales while I sang. The lesson just flew by as I really enjoyed it. After it was over, he gave me some books of music and asked me to practice them for the following week.

All the way home I thought: *What I have done? How do I get out of this one?* The expression: "in for a penny, in for a pound" again came to mind. I learned that the more you lie, the deeper the lie becomes.

I arrived home and Father asked how my piano lesson had gone.

"Fine," I replied, trying to change the subject.

How will I practice what I've been given? I thought.

The next day, I sat watching television when Father walked in. "When are you going to practice your piano music?" he asked. He switched off the television, which meant: *practice now!* There was no sense arguing with him, so I got up and took my music out of my case. I set it upright on the piano without saying a word.

"Oh, he's given you some new music to practice," Father said.

"Oh yes, he's moving me on to the next level," I replied.

"That's good, he must think you're doing well then," he said.

I didn't say anything, because I was getting deeper and deeper into more lies, so I just started practicing my scales, first playing them on the piano and then singing them.

"Are you supposed to be singing?" Father asked.

"Oh yes, Father, it's a new technique!" I replied. He never questioned it again.

Chapter Twenty-One

Solo Competition

My lie continued to grow especially because I sang with the school choir. When we went to competitions, my solos were at the same venue, just at a different time. I was able to do the choir work and then walk down to my solo competition.

I won quite a few singing competitions, so I would have to sneak my certificate and my cup into the house and then to school the next day. I locked them in my locker because they had the words 'Singing Competition' written all over them!

This all worked out fine for a while, until one of my singing competitions fell on a Saturday in Pontefract and the school choir was not going to that one. I was horrified. I would have to ask Father to take me, but how could I keep him out of the competition room?

I know, I thought, *I'll tell him he will make me nervous, and that I'll do better if he isn't in the room."*

Father agreed to take me, go for a walk and come back later. I hated not telling him the truth, but each day, week, and month that went by, I'd dug a deeper hole for myself.

The day of the competition arrived and Father drove me to the hall in Pontefract. He walked me to the doors and asked where the room was. We were taken down several corridors until we came to room 2021.

"I'm all right now, Dad, you can go now. I just need to register, sit down and wait until it's my turn," I said. I held my hand out to stop him from entering the room.

"Ok, I'll come back when it's finished," he said as he walked down the corridor.

What a relief! I thought.

I walked into the room and gave my papers to the registrar who logged me in and asked me to take a seat at the front. I walked down the aisle quietly, found my chair and waited for my turn.

One by one, the contestants got up and sang. Then, my number was called – 14! My heart raced as I walked up onto the stage. Once I started singing, my nervousness vanished. I finished my song and went back to my seat to wait for the competition to finish and the results to be given. There were fourteen more contestants to go. When they had all sung, the judges would need time to compare their assessments. That was always the slowest part - waiting - and I was never good at that!

"Quiet please! The judges are ready to announce the winners in reverse order," someone said. The senior judge stood up, started from the last place and worked forward.

Divine Intervention

I didn't hear my name until last. I was so excited that I had won! I hurriedly walked up the steps to the stage to receive my certificate and cup. As I turned to walk back down the stairs, I looked at the audience and there, in the back row, sat my father.

Oh, how my heart sank as I thought: *What will he do, now the game's up?*

Everyone congratulated me and asked where my parents were.

"My Dad's in the back," I said, and waved at him to come down.

He walked down to the contestants and their parents and I could hear people say that he must be very proud of me, to which Father replied: "Oh yes, I am."

After all the chatter, we walked out of the room and not one word was spoken. We got into the car and Father didn't say anything for about half an hour. Then he asked: "Why all the lies?"

"I wanted to sing and knew that you wanted me to play the piano. I knew I couldn't do both because we couldn't afford it!" I cried.

I went on to tell him about the young man, and how things had happened, and that I'd wanted to tell him but could never get him alone. When we pulled up onto the driveway, Father looked at me and said: "You will not go out of the house for one month - no television, no friends and no singing lessons. Just stay in, for not telling the truth. I will phone Mr. Spinks and explain why you are not going for a month, and then you can go back to your singing lessons instead of piano."

"Ok Dad, that's fine," I said quickly, before he changed his mind.

Underneath, I think he was so proud of me. Winning the competition probably influenced his decision.

I heard him talking about it in the kitchen with my mother and she was furious. Father said that he had dealt with it, and nothing more was to be said.

The month went by quickly. I used to spend time in my bedroom visualizing where I wanted to be. Other people would pop into my thoughts and have a chat.

Soon, I was again taking my singing lessons and everything was back to normal, only this time everyone knew what I was doing. It was a relief because I didn't like keeping things from my father. It made me feel guilty.

He never said another word about it. He knew that I must have suffered enough with my own guilt.

Chapter Twenty-Two

My Search for Stardom

*A*t fourteen, I set off one Sunday (not telling anyone where I was going) to audition for a part in a *Jack and the Beanstalk* pantomime. I got the part of the *Fairy Starlight* and the song I sang was *Climb Every Mountain* from *The Sound of Music*. When I arrived back home, Mother asked where I had been.

"To audition for a pantomime," I said.

"What do you want to do that for?" she asked.

"Because I want to, and by the way, I got the part of the *Fairy Starlight*, so there!" I replied.

"That's good!" Father said.

Singing with the school choir, singing lessons and competition work had paid off. It felt good to have a breakthrough on stage, so to speak. I never thought about how I was going to get to rehearsals, but good old Dad got me there once a week, twice a week for dress rehearsal and every night for the two weeks of the show!

Father had to get up at 4:30 in the morning to go to work and the show didn't finish until 10pm. He did that for me.

Both weeks of the show were sold out. My family and relatives came to see me on the last night of the show and they all burst into tears when I sang. *That was it*, I thought - *on my way to stardom!*

I sent in an application for *Opportunity Knocks*, not thinking I would even land an audition. A letter arrived, however, and I had an audition in Manchester on a particular Saturday. Mother was horrified, as I had not told anyone. Yet again, good old Dad was there to take me. I didn't become an overnight success this time, but it was a different experience.

Father always told us to go for what we believed in, because then, we would never live with regrets. I think I drove him mad as I took his comment literally, even at fourteen!

When my mother asked me what I wanted to do when I left school, I told her that I wanted to be a pop star. She looked at me and said: "You have to get a proper job like your brother and sister. You can either work in an office or a shop, you choose."

My brother was a motor mechanic. My sister worked in the post office but really wanted to be a nurse. Me? I still wanted to be a pop star. My mother said I wouldn't amount to much if I didn't get a proper job. "So put the idea of being a pop star out of your head!" she said.

It was so difficult with Mother. We never seemed to get along. All I ever wanted to do was sing, but she couldn't be positive or encourage me in any way. According to her, I was a difficult child - never doing as I was told and always fighting outside of school.

That part was true. The kids at school were more like acquaintances. I played with them but didn't feel connected to them. If I wanted to play, I would have to look for them, because they wouldn't come to me unless they needed something and that was usually homework.

I was a bright child and very creative. I used to like to write poetry and stories for homework and for fun. I was always given an'A' for my projects and they were put up on the board at school. I also liked to draw flowers. Along with the music and the singing, it was a very creative combination. Therefore, the kids at school would talk behind my back and call me names, unless they wanted help with their homework.

Although I was a rebellious child, I always behaved in school. I wanted to do well. I played piano in assembly and was the lead singer in the choir, singing many solos at concerts. I was the choir secretary, Captain at netball, Captain of the school swimming team, active in school field events, House Captain and, in my last year at school, I was a Prefect. The school awarded me a one- month holiday at Bewerley Park for my work, good attendance, excellent behaviour, positive attitude and leadership skills. I thought: *if my mother wouldn't support my singing, I'd work hard to become successful and famous.* The word *famous* was important to me as a child, because I wanted to show everybody that I was *Somebody.*

Mother used to laugh and say: "You? - Famous? I think you have your head in the clouds. Now get real and think about a proper job." This spurred me on to do my best to prove her wrong. One day, she would see and apologize to me. My school reports were excellent and even the headmaster said that I was 'born to lead.'

Because I was different from the other people at school (and put the effort in), I was considered strange. I was bullied because the teachers liked me and I did well. The kids would push and shove me in the corridors and call me names, but I would not retaliate at school. Once, six kids attacked me and the teachers came and pulled them off of me. Once out of earshot of the teachers, I said: "I'll see you outside of school tonight." So, Mother was right, I was always getting into fights.

Chapter Twenty-Three

Loving Cop

When I was at Junior at school, there was one dog close to my heart that didn't belong to us.

I came home from school one day to find that a new family had moved onto our street. It was a policeman (Mr. Bell), his wife, and their dog: *Cop*. I loved this black and tan Alsatian. He looked at me from a distance with those knowing eyes and wagged his tail every time he saw me. He seemed to know and understand me. I was drawn to him every time I passed. Then, one day I decided to walk over to him. I leaned over the gate to fuss at him and he fussed back, licking me as though he was my best friend.

As I played with him, Mrs. Bell ran out and said: "I wouldn't do that! He's not very friendly towards people. He's a police dog and that's why we put: *Beware of the dog* on the gate!"

Divine Intervention

"But he's friendly!" I protested.

"Well, I would rather you didn't lean over the gate, as he could bite you," she replied.

"I don't think so," I said. I pulled back to the other side of the gate because I could see that she was anxious. I left, went home and had my tea.

The next day, I came home from school and as I walked up the street, Cop jumped over the gate and ran towards me, wagging his tail and running around me. I sat on the ground and fussed with him. He rolled over on his back and I tickled his belly. I felt that I had found a long-lost friend, because he seemed to know me and understand what I wanted. Over the next few weeks, we bonded in such a way that he knew what time I would walk up the street. I spent time with him each day.

One day, when I got home from school, Mother was waiting for me.

"What are you doing, playing with Cop, when you have been told not to?" she asked with anger. "Mrs. Bell has been to see me. You have got to stop playing with that police dog!" she demanded.

It was no use trying to reason with her. She had her mind made up. I ran upstairs crying, shouting: "Why do you do this? You don't understand!" and slammed my bedroom door shut.

I locked myself in my room and refused to come down for tea. I didn't want to talk to anyone! I only unlocked the bedroom door to let my sister come to bed.

I got up for school the next day and as I walked down the street, Cop jumped over the gate to fuss with me. He snuggled up to me as though he knew what had happened. When I came home from school in the evening, he was nowhere to be found. I was sad that I had missed my friend.

We'd finished our tea and were still sitting at the table when we heard a bark at the back door. My mother opened the door and there was Cop, barking and snarling his teeth at her. I ran out of the door and threw my arms around him. He wagged his tail and rolled over onto his back as I tickled his belly. At that point, Mr. Bell turned up and said: "I'm sorry if he's caused you a problem."

"Oh, no," Mother said, "No bother at all!" I knew she was scared of Cop but she wouldn't let on. Mr. Bell took Cop home, and we all just looked at each other. Mother said nothing.

I went to school the next week and the same thing happened repeatedly, until one day Mr. and Mrs. Bell turned up at our house. I was told to go and sit in another room. There was a big discussion regarding Cop and me and even though the door was closed, I could hear every word. I was so scared that they'd stop me from seeing him, because I loved him so much. My heart was racing and the sheer anxiety caused me to have palpitations. I could hardly breathe. Just at that moment, the door opened and I was called to come into the kitchen.

Because everyone stared at me, I felt uncomfortable.

Father smiled and said: "It appears that you and Cop cannot be separated. We've kept you apart and you haven't been happy. Cop has been kept in, and he cries."

Just at that point, there was a bark outside the back door. The door opened and there was Cop. I ran and put my arms around him and he made funny noises that meant that he was happy to see me. I could see a small piece of rope dangling from his collar. He had chewed himself free.

"See what we mean? He's never been like this with anyone else. In fact, he hates other people!" Mr. Bell said. "Your daughter can come for walks with Cop and I'll show her how to handle him. When I'm satisfied, she can take him on her own. She'll be safe because he won't let anyone come near her or hurt her," Mr. Bell said sternly.

"Is that all right with you, Patricia?" Father asked.

"Oh, yes, please!" I said with excitement.

"That's all settled then. We will start tomorrow when you come home from school," Mr. Bell said. They left with Cop by their side. Cop kept looking back at me as though he knew it was going to be all right.

Over the next two weeks, I would come home from school, get changed and call Mr. Bell. He and I would walk with Cop over the fields and back. Cop would wait by our gate and not leave until he could see that I'd gone into the house. Then he would carry on to his home.

On the Friday of the second week, we were on our way back from the walk when Mr. Bell said: "How would you like to take Cop out on your own tomorrow?"

"I would love that, Mr Bell!" I said. As we arrived at my house, I bent down and gave Cop a hug, saying: "See you tomorrow!" I skipped to my house filled with excitement.

"What's up with you?" Mother said.

"I'm taking Cop out on my own tomorrow, Mr. Bell said I could." I replied.

"Are you sure you are up to it?" she asked with a negative tone.

"Of course I am!" I snapped. "Otherwise, Mr. Bell wouldn't have said I could!"

Why does she have to be so negative and put me down all the time? I thought. I hated her for that. She could never say anything good about me. I sometimes wondered why she gave birth to me. She really wanted a boy so I was a big disappointment to her when I arrived. I don't think she ever forgave me for that. She reminded me on a regular basis, that if her stillborn baby boy had lived, I wouldn't have been around.

Saturday came and I called to pick up Cop and take him for a walk on my own. I had his ball in my pocket to throw when we got to the field. He walked with excitement and kept looking up at me, nudging me so that I'd look down. We seemed to walk on forever as though nothing else mattered. It was as if everything was in slow motion where only the two of us were walking and playing. Everything else around us slowed down to a stop. It was an amazing experience.

I felt so close to Cop. He was my best friend. We would play for a while and then find somewhere to sit down. Cop would lie by my side. I would talk to him as though he were human and he would listen, moving his head from side to side with a knowing look.

Every day I spent with Cop was special. He was the only one who understood me and we couldn't be apart from each other. When Mother would interfere and make me stay in for something I hadn't done, Cop would come to the back door and keep barking until she let me out of the house. He would look at her and snarl. He seemed to know how she treated me, and let her know that he was not having any part of it.

We had such a bond, a special relationship that could not be broken. I loved every minute I spent with him. My world seemed so much brighter with Cop around. I loved him so much and he showed me love without asking for anything in return. He filled my heart with so much joy.

I went to school one particular day feeling anxious and upset, but didn't know why. During the day, I could feel pain in my kidneys. I felt sick. By about 3 pm, all my symptoms had disappeared. A real sense of sorrow came over me. I looked down and there was Cop, sitting by my side, looking up at me. Then he disappeared. I wanted to go home but I had to stay until 4 pm. The school bell finally rang and I grabbed my things and ran to Cop's house, but he wasn't there. I rushed to the back door and knocked, but no one was in. I felt a sense of pain in my heart as I rushed home and ran into the house. My parents were waiting for me. Father looked at me as though he had something to say, but didn't know how to say it.

"Where is Cop?" I cried.

"He passed away this afternoon at 3 pm from kidney failure," Father said.

"Oh no, he can't leave me!" I screamed. I ran out of the house and made my way up to the field and sat down where we used to sit.

"Oh Cop, where are you? I need you, don't leave me!" I said, crying for the loss of my best friend. I felt that I hadn't been able to say goodbye properly and give him a hug, but I remembered he had visited me at school to say goodbye at the moment of his passing. I had felt his pain all day at school, so I knew he had to go. However, the pain and sorrow I felt was beyond belief. I was devastated that I would never see him again.

Father came looking for me and found me sitting by the tree near the stream, where Cop and I used to spend so much time together. He sat down beside me, put his arm around me and said: "Come on, its time to go home." He stood up and held his hand out to pull me up.

We slowly walked home. He didn't say much, but I knew he could feel my pain. When we got home, my mother was waiting with tea on the table.

"Come and sit and have your tea," she said.

"I don't want anything to eat," I snapped.

"You've got to eat something!" she insisted.

"I don't want anything!" I cried and ran upstairs to my bedroom.

Everyone kept out of my way for the next few days. I couldn't eat or sleep. I couldn't stop thinking about Cop because I missed him so much. I'd never before felt this kind of pain and loss. It was as though my heart had been ripped out. I felt so much grief and sadness.

As time passed, the pain grew less but I still missed him. I stopped going to our special place, because I couldn't bear to be there without him. I withdrew from my family. I felt as though I was in a different place, and that they would never understand how I felt.

School and homework kept me busy. I immersed myself in my studies and blocked out everything that could make me happy, including my music. I refused to go to my singing lessons. I became someone I didn't recognize. It was as though I *wanted* to feel the pain. I didn't want to be happy because I didn't have Cop.

About a month later, I woke up on a Saturday morning and had this urge to go for a walk. I found myself retracing the steps that I took when I walked with Cop, and ended up by a tree near the stream. I sat down and started to cry, when I felt something touch me. I looked up and there was Cop, wagging his tail with his ball in his mouth. I was so pleased to see him. I was crying and laughing at the same time.

"Oh Cop, I love you!" I said, and he came around to lie by my side. I talked and talked to him. I had so much to say. He looked up at me knowingly. I realized that I hadn't lost him forever and I could come and spend time with him here, whenever I wanted. After about two hours, Cop disappeared. I got up and walked home with a little bit of joy in my heart.

After that, I took every opportunity to go to our special place and spend time with my best friend. He seemed to know that I was alone and that I needed help to get back to normal. Over the next two months he was there for me. Seeing him again, helped me heal the pain and understand that just because he had passed, it didn't mean that I would never see him again. He would always be in my heart. I would always have the memories of the time we spent together. No one could take that away from me.

I eventually went back to my music and singing. I didn't feel sad any more. I understood that Cop couldn't be with me all the time, and that my memories of him were special. I realized that no one would understand the bond that we shared. I also learned that I didn't need to go to our special place to see him. Sometimes he would appear in my bedroom when I was alone.

I called Cop my *little angel from heaven*. He had come at the right time in my life, when I felt that I couldn't cope and wished that I would die. He was the sunshine that had appeared from nowhere, and he chose to spend time with me. I felt honoured and special. His love was far greater than any I had ever felt before. Cop had an amazing impact on my life that I will never forget. I was so connected to him. I could feel his pain even when he took his last breath. Something special happened between us and it was difficult for people to understand. He seemed to know me from the inside out. Our relationship was so special. I would never forget him.

Chapter Twenty-Four

Fido Finds a Friend

*T*oday, looking back, I can say that animals have always responded to me. I visited a house recently, to do eight readings for a family. As I rang the doorbell, I saw the fire of a dragon in my mind's eye. A little dog came running to the door growling and snapping. The owner opened the door just slightly so she could see me with one eye. "Just a minute," she said. "I have to put the dog in another room because he bites everyone." I waited and then she let me in with no dog in sight.

I was put in the living room and, one by one, I did the eight readings. After I had finished, everyone came and sat in the living room and I was given a cup of tea. We were all sitting, chatting and drinking tea when I watched the little dog enter the room and gradually walk behind each person's chair so that no one could see him. My arm was dangling down the side of the chair where I was seated. I didn't move but just sat very still as I continued to chat. The dog got closer and closer. He sniffed my bag and my fingers and pushed my hand to stroke him, which I did. Still, no one noticed him. In the next breath, he jumped up on my knee, sat down on my lap and just let me stroke him.

It took about five minutes before anyone noticed that he was on my lap. He was happily absorbing my Reiki energy and loving it. It was the people that he lived with who were stressing him out. He just wanted peace and quiet. Once everyone noticed, they were flabbergasted. "He has never done that before with anyone. He just bites everybody," someone said.

"He obviously likes the Reiki energy," I replied. The dog was so calm and relaxed that he didn't want me to get up. "I have to go," I told him. So he jumped off my lap and went back into the kitchen as I left. I got a call about a week later from the dog's owner who told me that the dog had changed. He was very calm and didn't growl or bite anyone. It's amazing how energy healing helps to calm an animal.

The fire of the dragon (that I saw earlier) had been put out. Animals are like people. They want love and attention. They also take on the owner's personality. The anger was not within the dog but within the person. So, some TLC and healing showed the dog's real personality. Learning how to put the fire and anger out was so important for the dog to have peace and quality of life.

Chapter Twenty-Five

Sneaking Out in Style

My brother used to feel sorry for my sister and me. Mother was not as bad with him. He had started work and was earning his own money; therefore he could buy his own clothes.

The next Christmas was interesting. We all sat down and opened our presents. My brother had kept his presents for us until last.

"Go on then, open your brother's present," Mother said. My sister and I both looked at each other while we tore open the packages.

We both said at the same time: "Thanks brother, for the stockings and suspender belt."

"You're welcome," he said.

Mother threw a fit. "You shouldn't buy your sisters those sort of things, it's not right!"

"It's the 60's, Mother, not 1922!" he replied.

"You won't get to wear them, so don't think you will!" she said and stormed off. Little did she know that our brother had asked us what we wanted for Christmas, and we told him: stockings and suspender belts. He got into trouble for us, so that we could have some modern things.

All my friends had modern clothes, stockings and even makeup, but none of this was allowed at our house. I saved up my paper route money and bought myself some makeup, stockings, suspender belts, some winkle picker shoes and a couple of dresses. I left them at my friend's house, so that my mother wouldn't find them. When I went out with my friends, we would all meet up at Susan's house early. I would get changed, put on my makeup, and then we'd go out. When I was due to go home, I'd go back to Susan's place, get changed, take off my makeup and then go to my house. My mother never knew until years later when I'd left school. She went mad when I told her, but I didn't care. I cleared my conscience of the deceit that I had to go through just so I could be a normal kid.

Chapter Twenty-Six

I Wanted to Scream

When I was fourteen, in late July, something happened that would change my life.

It was Sunday afternoon. My dad wanted some cigarettes from the machine on the main road and asked me if I would go get them. I usually took the dog, but this particular day, I couldn't be bothered. I got to the machine, purchased the cigarettes and, as I turned, a van pulled up and an old man got out.

"Can you tell me where Pear Tree Avenue is?" he asked, as he walked toward me. I was just about to say 'no,' when he pulled out a gun, stuck it in my chest, and said: "Get into the car!"

My heart was pounding. I wanted to scream but couldn't. No one was around; not one soul was anywhere, which was unusual. When I got into his van, I thought

Divine Intervention

I was going to die. He locked me in the front seat, ran around to the driver's side, and drove off.

"Where are you taking me?" I cried.

"Stop crying and shut up or I'll kill you!" he said.

I sat quietly, watching where he was taking me and wondering if I could escape. My heart was racing faster and faster. I felt like I was inside my body but not. It felt real, but also like a dream. All I wanted to do was wake up. He took me beyond Clayton where there were trees and then reversed the van down a quiet track into the woods. I felt that this was my last moment on earth. He stopped the car and said: "Get in the back!" That's when I noticed a coloured crochet blanket in the back of the van.

"I won't tell you again, get in the back!" he said, as he pointed the gun at my head. I did as I was told, and was terrified at what was about to happen. He climbed into the back of the van and started unzipping his trousers. I pushed and fought with him with all my strength. He hit me and pushed me down, ripped my clothes and sexually assaulted me. I thought he was going to kill me. When he had finished, he climbed back into the driver's seat (holding my arm) pulled me back into the passenger's seat and then started the van. It was slippery and the van wheels were spinning.

"Get into the driver's seat and press the pedal while I push," he said. So I did. The car started to move and I kept pressing the pedal, thinking I could get away. I pressed harder and harder and the van moved faster, but then the engine stalled. He caught up with me as I tried to start the car again. I had watched my dad start the car so many times I thought I could do it. He dragged me out, threw me into the sludge, and ordered me to get back into the car or he would kill me. He pulled the gun out of his pocket and put it in my face. I quickly got back into the van.

My heart was pounding. I was sure I was going to die, and as those thoughts consumed me, I could see flashes of light. An angelic figured appeared and said: "You will be fine. All will be well. You have a long life ahead of you, don't worry." Then it disappeared.

I felt calmness come over me and everything appeared to move in slow motion. I could see the van in detail. I could also see the man very clearly, every nook, scar and mark. It was as though I had taken a picture and was looking at the full detail. I was not looking where we were going at this point, but absorbing the details in my mind. I had no idea that all these details (about the van and the man) would be the factual information that would lead to his arrest.

When the van stopped, he told me to get out. I jumped out and to my surprise; I was standing at the same shop where I had bought the cigarettes. He drove off and I ran all the way home.

As I ran in the back door, my mother shouted at me: "Where have you been?"

My dad said: "Look at her! What happened?"

"A man took me at gunpoint, drove up into the woods and raped me," I cried.

"I told you never to get into a car!" my mother ranted, as though she didn't believe me.

"I'm taking her down to the Police Station," Father said.

Once there, I had to give a full statement. The police phoned a doctor and arranged for him to examine me at home.

Divine Intervention

There was a chilled atmosphere when I got back to the house. I sat in the room and everyone looked at me. Not one word was spoken. Finally, Father said: "The doctor is coming to examine her, so everyone will have to go into the kitchen."

When every one moved, there was a lot of muttering, so I shouted: "Can you please stop talking about me?"

At that moment, there was a knock at the door and the doctor walked in. He examined me and confirmed, to my mother's horror, that yes, I had been raped. Her reaction?

"All these coming and goings with police cars. What will the neighbours think?" she asked.

She had great difficulty in showing love and emotion. I always remember what the doctor said to my parents in the kitchen: "They needed to watch me, because this experience could have an effect on me mentally and emotionally, and either I would hate having sex or become a sex addict." What an abnormal thing to say in the circumstances.

Chapter Twenty-Seven

Confronting the Rapist

After the doctor left, I was given some tablets and told to get a bath and get into bed. There was total silence in the house. Nobody said a word and you could hear a pin drop. I thought I was dirty and that no one loved me. No one showed me any love or cuddled me. That night, I felt so alone.

The next day, the police came to the house, showed me pictures, and drove me around to find the place where the man had taken me. The police said my detail of the van and the old man was amazing. Nevertheless, I could not find this old man in the pictures they showed me. Nearly two weeks passed and they still hadn't found him, so they told my parents that they wanted to put it on *Calendar* news with a Photofit picture of the rapist. Mother was horrified. She didn't want it to be on Yorkshire television

– what would people think? However, Father intervened and said that it was ok, if they had to do it.

The next day, the police turned up and told my parents that they had found the van. My description of the vehicle and the blanket in the back was so accurate. It was that blanket in the back that had been the breakthrough. They wanted to take me with them to identify the vehicle and the man.

The police drove me out to where the man lived. They told me not to worry because police and detectives surrounded the area. I identified the van and the blanket in the back. Then they knocked on the door and told the person who answered that they'd come to see their father. They quietly explained what it was about and the family shouted to their father to come down the stairs. The whole scene went into slow motion – the old man then slowly walked down the stairs.

When he was halfway down, I said: "That's him!"

He turned and looked at me. Then, he pulled a gun out of his pocket and shot himself in front of the police, his family and me. The police grabbed me, rushed me outside, and sat me down with a policewoman. She then drove me home and explained to my family what had happened. When she left, everyone was silent – not a word spoken except by my mother: "Go and get a bath and go to bed."

No emotion, feelings or love was shown at this time.

I got up the next day and the police turned up at the door. They wanted to show me some photographs again and asked if I could pick him out. I looked very closely and said: "That's him, but he's so much younger and with a beard."

The police thanked me for all my help and left. Mother walked up to me and, for the first time, tried to cuddle me. I pushed her away. "It's too late!" I said, and walked away.

Chapter Twenty-Eight

Rape and Abuse

*T*he woman's rape was shown to me like a video in my crystal ball. I saw her struggle with her husband as he raped her. I could describe his features in detail, along with what he was wearing at the time and exactly what had happened.

This helped me give the reading with sensitivity and feeling. It also gave my client confirmation that I knew exactly what had happened. The feeling and emotions that came out of that woman and the tears she shed were overwhelming.

No one would believe her, not even her parents. As far as they were concerned, she was married, so her husband could not rape her. They told her that she was just making it up to get out of her arranged marriage. For the first time, someone believed her and because

I could describe everything in detail, she felt relief. This helped her immensely and our working relationship continued to develop.

On another occasion, I read for a young woman and intuitively knew through my reading, that her husband had mistreated her and sexually raped her. She lacked confidence and felt dirty and degraded

My own experience with rape gave me a greater understanding about her situation. I counseled her and gave her Reiki healing sessions. After three months, she felt strong enough to stand up for herself and leave him. She filed for divorce, moved back to her parents' home and started a new life for herself. She continued her sessions for another eight months and gained confidence and strength within herself.

She trained in Reiki, did a lot of work on herself and went on to become a Reiki Master. Two years later, she met a new man, got married and now has three children. She once told me that without our counseling sessions, she would never have had the courage to leave her former husband and find a better life.

I told her that she had done it on her own. She had made the commitment to change her life. She had the willingness to release her resentment and forgive herself and her ex-husband so she could move on.

Today, I understand why I had to endure such trauma and why I had to experience the pain that I did.

I have worked with many people (like these women) over the last ten years who have been sexually, mentally or physically abused. Most cannot stand up for themselves.

Divine Intervention

Now, the greatest pleasure I can have is to watch a person who I have helped, go on to help others by becoming a counselor. If I can have a positive influence on just one person's life, then my own trauma at such an early age will have been well worth it.

Chapter Twenty-Nine

Not Your Average Movie

*M*y Father never said anything about the rape.
I think he found it difficult because he had to
live with the guilt all his life for sending me to the shop
for his cigarettes. I could feel his pain but we never spoke
about it. I knew that he cared a great deal about me and
what had happened and was angry with himself about it.
I always used to pick up his thoughts: *If only I had not sent
her to the shop. Why did this have to happen to her?*

This all happened during the holidays so I had time
to recover before going back to school. I didn't go out
much, just into our back garden. I didn't want to see or
talk to people, as I knew they would want to ask questions
and I wasn't ready to talk. I had to deal with this on my
own since nothing was offered to help me. There was no
counselling; therefore, I had to try to sort things out in my
mind, which was not easy.

Divine Intervention

One Saturday, Mother insisted that I go with my sister to the Saturday cinema. I really didn't want to go. As we walked to the cinema (which was about two miles from the house), I felt the other kids stare and talk about me. The trauma had heightened my senses and I could hear all of them saying: "That's the girl who got raped, isn't it?"

I turned to my sister and said: "I want to go home. They're all talking about me!"

"Oh come on! Mother said you had to go to the cinema!" She grabbed my arm and pulled me along.

My sister paid at the cinema and as we went inside, everyone looked at me as though I was an animal in the zoo. Being a mining village, everybody knew everything. Nothing slipped by. My rape was the highlight of the village's gossip, but nobody once gave any thought to how I felt about it. People love other people's misery but they don't know how much pain and suffering they cause for others.

At that moment, I hated everyone.

I knew that my parents were trying to be helpful, getting me out of the house and back to a normal life but I just didn't feel ready. I wanted to hide away with my shame.

At the cinema, the lights went out and the film began. I can't even remember what the movie was about. It felt like it was just somewhere in the distance. I could hear voices and a white light appeared to the side of the screen. Twelve men (dressed in white) walked out from the light. An angel was with them. Everything seemed to be in slow motion. I could feel myself sitting in my chair, but at the same time, I was floating up in the air to meet the angel and the twelve others. The angel welcomed me and the twelve people were introduced to me as "The Brotherhood". They blessed me and told me I would have a lot of work to do in the future, spiritually. Before that could happen, I would have to have life experiences that would not always be pleasant, but my soul would grow from them and I would become something special. They said I would travel with my spiritual work and would become a great healer, later in life.

"You are chosen as a special one," they said. Then, they disappeared back into the white light.

The angel put her arm around me and said: "Out of all these people, you are special. You can rise above them. I am with you to help you through this and on your journey." I watched her go back through the white light. At that moment, the light disappeared and I returned to my body with a sense of great peace and calm.

The film ended and we left the cinema for home. My sister asked if I was all right. "Yes," I said. After that, I never spoke a word about my experience in the cinema. I even wondered if it had been real. My mind questioned everything that I had seen. Father had always taught us to question things that we did not understand. He told us that if we couldn't fit it into anything normal, then it had to be an experience for us alone.

When we got home, I ran upstairs to my bedroom, still searching for answers for what had happened at the cinema. After about thirty minutes, the angel appeared again in my bedroom and said: "Do not question what you saw. It was real." Then, she disappeared.

Divine Intervention

I didn't speak to anyone about what had happened because I thought they would say that I had made it up. They would blame it on my trauma, or my own vivid imagination. It would be many years later, before I would speak to my father about it. We would talk for hours, exploring what was still so vivid in my mind. The trauma had made me 'see' more clearly. I could look at something for one second and describe every detail with perfect accuracy.

During the rest of the summer holiday, I never went out to play, preferring instead, to stay in the house or garden. I hadn't gone to my singing lessons for several weeks. Father said that it was time to try and get things back to normal. I agreed to go because he would drive me there and pick me up when I had finished. My mother phoned up my singing teacher, Mr. Spinks, and arranged for me to go the following week.

That day came and I felt fearful about going out, but I knew I would be going with my father. When we started out, Father took a turn that he usually didn't take. My heart began to pound and panic set in.

"Where are you going and why are we going this way?" I asked.

"We are going to your singing lessons, why?" he said, looking puzzled. By this time, I was in tears as we pulled up outside the singing teacher's house.

"What's the matter?" Father asked, turning towards me.

"The man who raped me – that was the route he took." I replied. Father put his arms around me and held me for a moment. Neither of us said a word.

"Shall we go inside?" he asked. "Come on, I'll walk you to the door."

I got out of the car, Father opened the gate and we walked up the path to the front door. As we approached, Mr. Spinks appeared to let us in. He asked me to go into the music room and sit down, which I did. They obviously wanted to talk. I heard the front door slam shut as Mr. Spinks walked into the room. He walked straight over to the piano and started my lesson. We first practiced the scales and then the song that I was practicing for a competition in September. At the end of the lesson, Mr. Spinks phoned my father to come and collect me. While we were waiting, he told me that my voice had improved and sounded different: 'more angelic' were the words he used. I thought about my experience at the cinema and wondered if that had changed my voice in some way.

My father arrived and as I was leaving Mr. Spinks said: "See you next week."

"OK, thanks," I replied, and ran to the car. As we drove home, we talked about my lesson and the competition in September. It seemed like my panic session had never happened. When we got home, I jumped out of the car and ran into the house. Everyone was trying to be normal but at the same time it made me feel uncomfortable. It was obvious that there had been a big discussion about me. Everyone was making a big effort not to put his or her foot into it.

After about thirty minutes, I couldn't take it any longer and said: "I'm tired, I'm going to get a bath and go to bed." Everyone said goodnight and I went upstairs.

Divine Intervention

My mother had already been up and drawn the curtains, so I went straight to bed.

Before I could lie down, six circular-shaped objects came flying into the room from nowhere. They were all different colours, and together they were just like the colours of the rainbow. As they flew around the room, they made me laugh. In response to my laughing, they made noises and it felt like I had six naughty children.

Suddenly the stairs door opened and my mother shouted: "What's going on up there?"

"Nothing, Mother," I replied.

"Just get to sleep," she said as she shut the door. When I turned to look at the flying balls, they were gone. Just for those few minutes, I had forgotten my problems. I pulled the covers up to my head and went to sleep.

Chapter Thirty

Back to School

The summer holiday was just about over, and I had to go back to school. I knew that everyone would be looking at me, pointing fingers and whispering about the rape. I really didn't want to deal with that.

Father had taken the day off work so he could drive me to school and talk to the Headmaster. That was embarrassing because it made me stand out even more. I knew everyone would be looking and whispering as we drove past. I just knew what it would be like.

At fourteen, I felt like I was all grown up. You just didn't let your parents drive you to school. That was a downer. I knew Father meant well, but I really wanted to go to school as usual; however, he insisted we go in the car.

As we drove up the main road, I saw everyone walking up the hill to the school. It was a mixed school, so there were both boys and girls looking at our car. Everyone was pointing and whispering. I could hear their voices in my head.

The playground was full. As we drove through the gates into the schoolyard, every single person focused on us. Their voices were jumbled in my head. I looked down at the car floor rather than through the window. My heart raced and sank at the same time and I started to panic.

Father parked the car and asked: "Are you all right?"

"No! I just want to go home!" I said.

"Come on, we're here now, and you'll have to walk in sometime," he said.

I knew he was right, so I got out and we walked to the Headmaster's office. He seemed to be waiting for us, so my parents must have arranged the meeting in advance. I was directed to the next room with the school secretary, while my father followed Mr. Haigh into his office. The secretary was not comfortable. I could feel her anxiety on top of my own and I could hear every word my father was saying.

It was like being there but not. I kept getting pictures in my head - like watching a movie of what was happening in the Headmaster's office. The conversation seemed to go on forever as people came and went into the secretary's office. They seemed very uncomfortable with me being there. No one knew what to say. They found it difficult just to say hello. My anxiety and panic mounted as my father appeared with Mr. Haigh, who smiled at me.

"When the school bell rings in a few minutes, you can go straight to your classroom Patricia," he said.

"Thanks. See you later, Dad," I said.

Divine Intervention

"I'll pick you up tonight," he said. I walked down the long corridors to the classroom. When I entered the room, there was no one in sight, (not even the teacher) so I sat down at my desk and waiting for everyone else to arrive.

My heart raced as I anticipated each person's reaction. Panic set in as the door opened. In came the teacher, Mr. Dollan, with his hands full of books and files.

"Hello Patricia, can you come and help me with these books and things? Please put one of these files on everyone's desk," he said.

"Yes, I can do that," I said. I could feel his tension, but at the same time, I knew that he was trying to act normal. I did what he asked and then returned to my desk. The school bell rang and all the corridors filled with people rushing around. The door flung open and the rest of the class filed in.

"Come on, sit down quietly," Mr. Dollan said. As each person sat down, a silence came over the room. People looked over their shoulder at me and whispered to the person next to them. Even my (so-called) friends who sat beside me were whispering to each other. By this time, I was ready to run out of the room, when Mr. Dollan shouted: "Quiet please. Let's get the class register done and then, we can get on with some work." Everyone sat up and started to pay attention. Mr. Dollan was a strong disciplinarian and we all jumped when he spoke.

He called the class register and then got on with the work. I still felt that people were watching me and whispering and my friends did the same. I felt so alone and helpless. I just wanted the day to be over. Our break came and we had to go outside. Nobody spoke to me (including my friends), but everyone kept looking and whispering. I could hear every word they said: "That's the girl who got raped. Did you hear about it? It was all over the newspapers!" My exceptional hearing had become my worst nightmare.

I just wanted to run away, so I started to walk quickly towards the school gates. I felt like I was in another world. I could see a white light. The people in the school playground faded into the distance and a feeling of calm came over me.

"Stay and see the day through. You will see it change," a voice said. I stopped walking, as someone grabbed my arm.

"Where are you going?" my friend Susan asked.

"Nowhere," I replied.

"Why not come over here with us?" she suggested.

"Ok," I said, as we walked over to join the others. The conversation was strained and I could feel the tension. They were dying to ask me questions but, at the same time, they didn't dare.

The school bell rang and we walked back into the room for our next lesson. I managed to get through the day but was filled with tension. Everyone was whispering about me. Since they didn't know what to say, they avoided me like the plague.

The final school bell rang and I rushed out looking for my father. I ran to the car, jumped in, and said: "Come on, let's go!"

"What's the matter?" he said as he started the car.

"Oh nothing, I just want to get home," I said, catching my breath. After that, we sat in silence waiting for the other to say something, but neither of us did. When my dad pulled in the drive, I jumped out and ran into the house.

"What's the rush?" my mother asked.

"Oh, no rush," I said, as I dashed upstairs to change out of my school clothes.

"Your tea is ready," she shouted from the bottom of the stairs. I knew that was a command, so I ran downstairs to the table.

My parents sat at the table discussing what was happening in the world. My sister and brother were eating and talking about what my brother was doing, and I just sat sipping my tea, wishing I could be somewhere else.

Not a word was spoken about my day at school. It appeared that everyone was avoiding the subject.

After tea, I did my homework, went upstairs, got a bath and went to bed. I didn't need to ask to go to bed these days. I just wanted to be out of the way so everyone could talk normally.

My father only took me to school that first day. After that, I went on my own.

It was not an easy time at school because everyone found it difficult to talk to me. I could feel their anxiety and hear their thoughts. I got through the first week without incident, although my frustration was building and there was nothing I could do about it. I felt so isolated and alone.

My family wanted me back at school and back to normal, but what is normal for someone who has been raped and sexually assaulted? You never heard about things like that on television or in the newspapers. Living in a mining village, everyone knew everyone else's business.

Divine Intervention

What had happened to me was unheard of, so it was the highlight of everyone's gossip without any consideration for my feelings.

Chapter Thirty-One

Spontaneous Combustion

The second week at school was full of tension and emotion. Everyone still huddled in corners whispering, and comparing notes on what they had heard and what they knew. I could hear every single word.

By the time Thursday came, I had really had enough. It was lunchtime and raining outside so we were allowed to stay indoors. I ate in the school canteen and walked back to the classroom. In my second year at the school, the Education Department had merged the boys' and girls' schools together to create Thurnscoe High School. Things are not straightforward when that happens. People are noisier and it's not easy when you are hearing their thoughts and feeling their emotions. As I got to the classroom and opened the door, my friends were talking to some boys. They were horrified that I walked in right at that crucial moment when they were talking about me and wanting all the gory details. At that moment, I looked at my friends and flipped out. In other words: *I saw red!*

"How could you?" I shouted as I ran after them. I had the strength of an ox. I threw my friends over the desks as the boys grabbed for me. I grabbed them instead and one by one, flung them to the other side of the room. At that moment, the teacher came rushing in, took my arm and asked what had happened.

I burst into tears saying: "I came in and they were all talking about me and what had happened to me when I got raped. They wanted to know all of the gory details! Why do they have to do this to me, haven't I gone through enough?" I cried.

The teacher hurriedly took me to the Headmasters' office and sat me down with a cup of tea, while the teacher explained to the Headmaster what had happened.

"Are you all right, Patricia?" Mr. Haigh enquired.

"I am now," I said wiping the last tear from my face.

"I want you to go home for the rest of the day while I deal with this," he said. "Mrs. Moran is free this lesson, so we'll get her to take you home with a letter for your parents. Go and wait in my secretary's office, and we'll get things sorted out," he said, as he shouted for his secretary to come into the room. I left his office, sat in the secretary's room and waited.

There was a lot of coming and going into the Headmaster's office and the secretary was back and forth typing letters. Suddenly, Mrs. Moran appeared and said: "Come on Patricia, I'll take you home."

It felt like I'd been sitting in the secretary's office forever.

Divine Intervention

Mrs. Moran was silent as she drove me home. When we arrived, she quickly got out of the car and said: "Just wait there until I have spoken to your mother." I was angry. Yet again, here was another conversation behind my back.

Suddenly, my mother appeared and shouted: "Come on in the house!" I jumped out of the car and ran inside, up the stairs to my bedroom and Mrs. Moran left to go back to school.

I thought Mother would come upstairs and tell me off, but she left me alone and not a word was spoken. I heard Father come home from work and there was a great discussion downstairs. I could hear every word they said about what had happened, and why it had happened, and what they were going to do with me.

I heard footsteps on the stairs. Dad popped his head around the door and asked: "How are you?"

"I'm ok," I muttered.

"You are to take the rest of the week off from school while Mr. Haigh deals with things," he said.

"That will make things worse!" I cried.

"No, it won't," he said with strength in his voice.

"Now come down stairs and get your tea," he said, patting my head as he left the room.

I went downstairs and sat at the table. Things were a little strained, to say the least. Mother was trying to be normal but every word and gesture seemed insincere.

I hated being at home because there was not much going on when everyone was at school. I didn't return to class until the following Monday. While I was off, I tried to keep out of my mother's way so there would be no confrontation. I sat in the garden looking at the faces in the clouds, wishing I were somewhere else. Mother never could show any feelings or emotions so it was difficult for me to have that kind of relationship with her.

All through this time, it was very difficult for me. I continued my singing lessons but I felt like a robot. There was no feeling or emotion in my singing. I went through the motions to keep my parents happy, but my heart was not in it.

The days off from school and the weekend passed without event. Everyone was trying to be normal, yet it was like a pantomime with each person trying to be someone else. I felt as though I was on the outside looking in.

Monday came and I walked to school as normal. As soon as I got inside the school gates, the teacher came up to me and rushed me off to Mr. Haigh's office saying: "Mr. Haigh would like to see you before you go to your classroom."

He sat me down in the office and left. Five minutes later, Mr. Haigh walked in and sat down.

"How have you been these last few days?" he asked.

"Ok," I replied.

"Well," he said, "I've dealt with the situation and no one will be asking questions or bothering you again," he said thoughtfully.

"What's happened?" I asked.

"Well, the boys in question have been disciplined and a letter was sent home to all parents, with special letters to your friends' parents. Your friends were suspended from school for two days, and I can guarantee that no one in this school will bother you, so if for any reason they do, you let me know immediately!"

I was horrified. They would all hate me and look for revenge.

"You can go to your class now before the bell rings," he said.

"Thank you," I said, and left for my classroom.

Mr. Haigh was a strong disciplinarian and everyone respected him. That didn't stop me though, from feeling frightened and vulnerable. I arrived at the classroom before anyone else and rushed to my desk. I thought about what everyone would think of me. Then, the bell rang and there was a rush of students in the corridor. The door flung open and everyone piled in. There was total silence. I felt everyone's thoughts and feelings, and at that moment, I knew that they felt awkward with me.

Suddenly, the classroom door opened and Mr. Dolan came in. "Ok everyone! Let's get the class register done, and then we can get on with some work," he said briskly.

When the register was completed, we started to work. It was strange because we had never worked like this before. We were given tasks, split into groups, and made to work together so people had to talk to me, even though the conversations were stilted. Mr. Dolan would come by, get involved and (in a subtle way), get people to bring me into the conversation.

The whole day was the same. With each lesson, it became easier for everyone to relax. We were wrapped up with this new way of working. No one was thinking about me. That made it easier because I didn't have to listen to each person's thoughts.

Divine Intervention

After a couple of weeks, everything seemed to get back to normal. Even my friends started to come around. That was such a relief for me. It had been bad enough going through what I had with the abduction, rape and sexual assault, but to relive it at school was a nightmare. There was no counselling (or the doctor couldn't be bothered with it). I had to deal with it myself, which meant that I needed someone to talk to. I couldn't talk to my mother, so I had no one.

It wasn't easy for me, but it also was not easy for my father. He had to live with the fact that he had sent me down the street for a pack of cigarettes and that I had gotten into trouble. He couldn't do anything about it or take the pain away. In other words, he couldn't make it better. My father carried that guilt for the rest of his days. I didn't know or understand this until later in my life. I do know one thing: he never asked me, ever again, to go down the street and get him a pack of cigarettes. Also, he always tried to get me to take the dog everywhere I went.

Chapter Thirty-Two

Why is This Happening to Me Again?

About three months after I had been raped, I found myself in a similar situation. A man who my family knew very well seemed to think that once I had been raped, I was fair game. He managed to get me alone, played with my private parts, and then forced himself on me to have sexual intercourse. I told him I didn't want to, but he held his hand over my mouth so I could not make a sound. He was older and stronger and although I tried to push him away, I couldn't. I could not tell my mother, because she would not have believed me. It was someone she thought very highly of. She would not have believed that he could do such a thing. I began hating myself, because I could not stop it. I felt dirty and didn't want to live. My personality changed. I did not want to go out. I did not want to be on my own where this person could take advantage of me. I began to hate people touching me or even being near to me. It made my skin crawl.

My fear of this person grew. He seemed to follow me without me knowing it. He would appear from nowhere (when no one was around), and pull me into a quiet place to have sex. That was all it was, with no feeling. My body was limp with disgust and fear.

How could anyone do this? I did finally tell my mother what was happening but she said that I was lying and did not want to hear anymore about it. So, what could I do? The pain I felt and the horror of what was happening to me did not matter to anyone.

Could anything else happen to me?" At this time, I was very depressed and couldn't wait to leave home and move away from everyone.

This kept happening over a twelve-month period until he found himself a new girl friend. Then, he reluctantly left me alone. My fear of men was such that I couldn't stand any man to be near me. It changed my behaviour towards men in a way that I could never explain.

The feeling of fear and disgust never left me. I didn't know at the time how much these experiences would influence my future relationships.

At the time of this encounter, a 'Being' appeared to me and said: "Remember your body is only a vessel. It is your soul's growth that matters."

I was angry when I received that message because my pain was so severe. I wanted to know how they could allow this to happen to me? Surely, no one had to go through all of this in one lifetime, let alone before I had even left school. The scars felt like daggers through my heart. I wasn't sure I could forgive anyone ever again for the pain that I felt, especially my mother, for not believing me.

Chapter Thirty-Three

Praise from the Headmaster

*A*t school, despite the difficulties I had experienced, my reports were always excellent. This drew attention to my creativity and leadership skills. My determination to succeed was always at the forefront of my mind. I loved being in charge of things and bringing people with me. I loved making a success of whatever I was doing and watching others develop too. My greatest satisfaction was seeing others grow and develop in what they were doing. When I saw people struggling, I would help them as much as I could, and never ask for anything in return. Life is strange though, because no one ever did that for me. When I was young, I couldn't understand why others didn't see in me what I could see in them.

One day, my head teacher said to me: "You will leave this school and go on to make a difference in this world, as you care about others more than you care about yourself. That's a special quality in a person."

I turned red with embarrassment and couldn't respond.

"You see, Patricia," Mr. Haigh said, "I've left you speechless. You don't see the effect you have on others, despite how difficult life's been for you. You're a girl of substance and you don't even see it. That's why you've been awarded the Student Award this year. Your prize is four week's holiday at Bewerly Park. You deserve this," he said smiling.

"You know, Patricia, some of the other students are jealous of you, because you put your heart and soul into everything you do. That's why they treat you differently."

"Jealous of me, sir?" I questioned.

"Yes, Patricia, jealous of you," he replied.

"But I give them no reason to be jealous!" I said, puzzled.

"Patricia, you do well at school. You're Captain of netball, swimming and rounders. You're Head of House, Choir Secretary, lead singer in the choir *and* you play piano in assembly *and* you have good results in all subjects *and* you have excellent school reports!" he said.

"Sorry sir, but I don't understand. I don't brag to people or rub things in their faces."

"I know you don't, Patricia. You have a great deal to learn about people and the way they view things. To them, you're already successful. You find it easy to study. They see you as being independent and able to deal with anything that life and school can throw at you. In other words, they want to be like you, but they can't," he said.

"They want to be like me, Sir? I can't imagine why, as my life isn't easy," I replied.

"You will understand one day, Patricia," he said, as he walked off toward his office.

This encounter with the headmaster had me thinking for weeks. *Why would anyone want to be like me? Nobody likes me!* I kept thinking.

During this time, I started my menstrual cycles, which, at first, affected my ability to see. I learned that this was the only time I could not see, hear, sense, smell and feel things. I didn't know why, but it always happened at that time.

Chapter Thirty-Four

My Spirit Guide — Grey Cloud

One Saturday afternoon, I was walking up in the fields. The sun was shining and a gentle wind was blowing. I could feel the sun on my back, the breeze through my hair and a sense of peace and tranquillity. I came to the stream, sat down and watched the sun create stars and rainbows on the water. I took off my shoes and socks and sat dangling my feet in the cool water. I had never felt so much peace and calmness. The breeze was blowing through the trees and I could hear the rustle of leaves in the wind. I felt like I was in another place. Everything started to move in slow motion. The animals, birds, trees and the stream all slowed down and a beautiful rainbow appeared slowly across the sky.

Divine Intervention

I couldn't believe my eyes. I kept rubbing them and looked again, but I kept seeing the same thing. I wasn't scared. I could just see the beauty and feel the stillness of time.

Am I in another place or has time stood still? I thought. Everything was so amazing. All I could feel was perfect peace, where no one else existed or mattered. It was a feeling of being at one with myself: here and there, at the same time. It was like watching two movies simultaneously: One movie where I actually was (reality) and the other movie where time stood still. It was so amazing. Nothing like this had ever happened to me before.

Is this real? I thought.

"Of course it's real," a voice said, and a face appeared in the stillness-of-time picture.

"Who are you?" I asked.

"I am your Guardian through this part of your life," he answered

"What's your name?" I asked.

"Grey Cloud," he replied.

Oh yes, I thought.

At that moment, the clouds in the sky formed into an old Indian face in full headdress. "Grey Cloud is my name," he said with such pride.

"Oh, I believe you," I stuttered, as I looked at the beautiful picture he'd created in the sky.

"You always question everything, Patricia," he said.

"I know. I have to be sure of what and why, when and how, to find out whether or not things are real. That's not wrong, is it?" I asked puzzled. I was also a little angry that someone, or something, would question me, as I had enough of that from my mother.

"It's not wrong, Patricia, but it is time to give you some understanding of things," he replied.

"What understanding?" I asked.

"The time is right for you to have some understanding. Your headmaster spoke to you didn't he?" he asked.

"How did you know that?" I questioned.

"We watch and see what happens, that's how," he replied.

I am talking to myself! I thought.

"But you're not, or I wouldn't be here," he replied. "Look, Patricia, it is time to talk to your father, and tell him about your experiences. He can help you now," he said.

"But my mother won't let me talk to him! She always comes in and sends me off somewhere else, so I can't spend time with him" I said.

"Don't get frustrated, Patricia. We will create the opportunity for you to talk to your father when the time is right. You are very close to that time," he replied.

"How did you know that I was feeling frustrated?" I asked.

"Just like you can feel the feelings and emotions of others, I can feel yours," he answered.

"Oh."

"Patricia, you are a special child who still has a lot to learn. Your answers will come bit by bit at the right time. You have no idea how special you are right now, but you will learn," he said, disappearing into the sky.

"But… Don't go! I have so many questions!" I said, pleading for him to stay.

"I know. You have many questions. They will be answered in the fullness of time. Remember what I have said. I have to go now," he said, his voice disappearing into nowhere.

When I looked around, I was back by the stream in what I called my reality, and the other picture had gone.

I sat for a while, pondering over what had happened. I wasn't sure what to make of it.

Suddenly, I looked at my watch. What had felt like ten minutes had, in fact, been three hours. I jumped up and ran all the way home. I didn't want to be late for tea or I would get another scolding from my mother.

I ran to the gate and then walked down the path to the back door. As I walked in, every one was just sitting down at the table.

"Just in time for tea," Father said.

"Where have you been all this time?" Mother snapped.

"Oh, just out walking," I told her.

"You and your walks!" she replied.

"Oh, leave the girl alone and let's have our tea in peace!" Father said, sternly.

Mother huffed, muttered under her breath, sat down and we all tucked into our tea.

I could see that Mother was curious about where I'd been and that she was looking for an opportunity to start a fight. I avoided looking at her, so that she couldn't make eye contact with me, and therefore wouldn't be able to ask me any questions. Not that she would believe me, even if I told her the truth, so it was better to say nothing.

As soon as I'd finished my tea, I jumped up from the

table and headed for the room to watch TV, so that I'd be out of the way. Although I was watching TV, my mind was on what had happened that day, up in the field by the stream.

Was it real, or just a dream? I wondered. I could not rationalize anything in my head to prove that it was false, but I was getting tired of trying to work it out.

I'd been watching TV for about an hour, when Mother came into the room. She said it was late, time to get a bath and go to bed. It wasn't worth arguing with her, even though it was only 7pm, so I got up and went upstairs. I was so tired from the day's events that I just couldn't keep my eyes open, and quickly fell asleep.

Chapter Thirty-Five

Ready to Leave Home

When I got up the next morning, Mother was in a bad mood, grouching about everything, so I tried to be quiet. But that didn't work.

"Where did you go yesterday?" she snapped.

"I told you, I went for a walk up to the field."

"I don't believe that for a minute!"

"I did go for a walk, by myself, up to the field!" I said, anxiously.

"I don't believe you. You were gone for hours," she snapped, looking at me with disbelief.

"But I did go for a walk by myself. I just lost track of time!"

"It's not normal. You are a strange child," she said.

"Why is it you always have to turn everything into me being a strange child?" I cried, pushing my chair away from the table and heading for the door.

My mother grabbed my arm, and said: "I have *not* finished with you!"

I pulled my arm away. "Yes, you have. I am off to school!" I said, and ran out of the house.

As I walked to school early, I wondered why she treated me like that. I hadn't done anything wrong!

I had tried doing what Father had asked me to do, but nothing was getting any better. I knew when I got home from school that I would be in trouble, but I didn't care anymore. All I wanted to do was run away from home.

The day at school passed without incident, and the school bell rang for us to go home. On the way there, I bumped into my sister, Angela. "You wait until you get home. You'll be in trouble!" she said, with a smirk on her face.

That was it for me. A rage built up inside of me. I turned towards her and hit her across that smirky face of hers. We ended up fighting and I made her nose bleed. She ran off shouting: "I am going to tell my mother! Just you wait until you get home!"

"Oh, get lost!" I replied. I just couldn't care about what happened, as I was already in trouble anyway. I wandered the streets, delayed getting home, and thought about how I could pack my bags and run away. I didn't want to be at home anymore. I just wanted to get away.

I found a bus shelter and sat there thinking until it was dark. I was hungry, but I didn't care anymore. I just didn't want to go home. People kept looking at me while they were waiting for the bus or walking by. It was beginning to get cold and I sat in the bus shelter, crying. It was about 9 pm. I didn't know where to go next to get warm, when a car pulled up. Father got out.

"What are you doing here, Patricia?" he asked.

"Nothing. I just don't want to go home." I said.

He walked towards me and sat down.

"You can't sit here all night, it's dark and getting cold," he said, putting his arm around me.

"I've had enough. I can't live in the same house anymore!" I cried.

"Your mother tries, Patricia, she just doesn't understand everything," he said.

"She hates me! She just wants to make my life miserable!" I sobbed.

"Come home and get something to eat, and then sleep on it until the morning," he said, pulling me up from the seat and cuddling me.

"Is Mother going to go on at me again?" I asked.

"No. Just come home, and we can sort things out," he said, opening the car door and helping me into the passenger seat.

"Ok," I said wiping the tears from my eyes.

We arrived home, got out of the car and walked in through the back door. There was complete silence in the house. You could have heard a pin drop.

"Come on, Mother, give the girl her tea," my dad said, looking at her. I could see by the look on her face that she was ready to blow a fuse, but she got my tea out of the oven and placed it on the table without saying a word.

I was so hungry I gobbled down my food. "Slow down Patricia, no one's going to take it away!" Father said from across the table.

I finished my tea and there was so much tension in the

kitchen that I got up and went upstairs, leaving everyone else downstairs to have a family conference about me.

The next few days were a little tense, to say the least. There were long silences and strange looks. I felt as though I wasn't wanted. The only person talking to me was Father.

In a quick quiet moment, he turned to me and said: "Don't worry; it will have all died down in a few days."

Those few days seemed like a lifetime to me. A minute felt like an hour. The whole family, apart from Father, didn't speak to me.

Chapter Thirty-Six

Granddad Appears at His Funeral

T̲he turning point came with a knock on the door during the night, along with a lot of voices and some commotion downstairs. I could hear what they were saying. My grandfather had passed away.

The next week was spent focusing on my grandmother and the funeral, so no one cared what I was up to. I felt numb and wasn't sure what everything meant. I got Father alone and asked him if I'd see my granddad again

"No, Patricia, he died, and he's gone to a better place," he replied.

"What place?" I asked him.

"He's gone to heaven, just like Jesus," he explained.

"You mean, I can't say goodbye to Granddad?" I asked, puzzled.

"You can in your heart," he said, putting his arm around me. As he held me, I felt his pain and grief. It was so great that I didn't ask him any more questions.

The day of the funeral came and all the family got together in their best suits. They looked more like they were going to a 'do', rather than a funeral.

People were crying and leaning on each other's shoulders. I stood beside Father and asked him: "If Granddad has gone to a better place, why are people crying?"

"They are just feeling sad because they loved him and won't see him again," he replied.

"But why can't they see him? I can. He's standing over there, smiling at me," I said, looking puzzled.

"You can see him, Patricia?" My dad looked at me.

"Yes, look, he's over there by the table. Can't you see him? He's waving at me. He's not gone," I replied.

"Don't say this to anyone else, or they'll get upset. Not everyone can see what you can see," Father said.

"OK," I replied.

"We'll talk some other time," Father said, as he walked off to talk to his brothers.

I kept thinking how could Granddad be gone, if I could still see him? That question stayed with me all day, but I kept quiet, as Father had requested. I felt happy that I could see my granddad and that he hadn't gone. This puzzled me for days.

Father didn't say anything for weeks, but I didn't mind. I could feel his pain and emotion, and I knew he needed time for himself. His mother had become quite demanding after the funeral and Father was doing all of her errands for her. I understood that he didn't have time for me.

For about two weeks after the funeral, I would go to my bedroom and sit on my bed, just thinking. My granddad would appear, sit on my bed and talk to me. I was close to him, and it brought me great comfort that I could still talk to him. After two weeks, he stopped visiting. I didn't see him again for about six months. Then, he would just pop in now and again to see if I was ok. I wasn't scared. I felt at ease. It was my granddad after all. Everyone had stopped talking about him and that made me sad. Being able to see him and talk to him were special moments, just for me. I didn't tell anyone, because I thought he or she would just get upset. Anyway, no one would have believed me.

Within a short time after my granddad died, we lost my mother's mum and father. I was close to my grandmother. She never criticized me, and used to tell my mother to "leave the girl alone." My grandmother was such a lovely person, and so understanding. She was the person in the village who everyone came to see. She would sort out some herbs for them and tell them what to do. She was like a nurse to everyone. I often used to wonder why my mother wasn't more like her.

The same thing happened at my grandmother's and grandfather's funeral: I saw each of them there, smiling.

Grandmother came, put her arm around me, and whispered in my ear: "You will make good in your life, Patricia, and don't let anyone tell you any different. I have to go, but I'll be back to see you now and again. Remember my words," and then she disappeared.

Everyone was crying and upset, but I felt so happy that I had seen her.

Divine Intervention

"What are you smiling about?" Mother snapped, as she wiped the tears from her eyes.

"Nothing, Mother, I just don't know what to do, or say," I replied. I could feel her pain. These were sad days, with everyone crying and feeling anguish.

What I couldn't understand was when people die, if they are going to a better place, why aren't people happy for them? This puzzled me a great deal. We had learned this at Sunday school and my mother used to go on about it all the time.

If only they could see what I can, they wouldn't be unhappy, I thought.

Chapter Thirty-Seven

Seeing Spirits

*M*y workroom is set with blue light that shimmers over my crystals, angels, fairies, and Buddhas and creates images and pictures on the walls and ceiling.

My students sit in a circle, creating their pure light energy. I talk them through meditation and watch them to make sure that everyone is all right. The first thing to change is the energy – they feel the heat build up. Then, the wispy white mist flows around them and forms into the shape of spirits behind their chairs. Only I can see as they all have their eyes shut. They just feel and see inwardly with their third eye. The first spirit to form is a Buddhist monk who looks at me with great peace and knowledge. Then others emerge and their message is always the same: one of love, nurturing and support.

Divine Intervention

Many of my students have been with me for 6 months or more, from all walks of life. I have prepared the healing room in advance and opened up the energy. The group gels and works together extremely well, charging the energy that has opened up for them. There is a great sense of warmth and peace and the room temperature goes up dramatically as we speak. Their visions in meditation get clearer as the weeks go on and their feelings of inner peace and knowing get stronger. It is wonderful to watch people grow from within, clear out the negativity from the past and find their own peace, balance and harmony.

PART THREE

Chapter Thirty-Eight

An Angel's Voice

The Beatles were popular during this time and I loved their music. In fact, I loved all of the 60's music. I got a paper route and worked every morning (and weekends) to make money to buy records. I would play them, learn the words and sing to my heart's content. When my parents were out, I used to turn the volume up and sing into the mirror and pretend I was a star. Music kept me going. I loved to sing and always felt good when I did. Somehow, it lifted my spirits whenever I felt down. All I wanted to do was to sing in a group. I used to drive Father mad by repeating a song, over and over again.

When the Beatles were coming to Sheffield City Hall, I really wanted to see them, and so did my friends at school. Father said: "If you earn the money and get the tickets, I will take you and bring you back." So, I worked and earned more money, and my friend's dad got us all the tickets. I was so excited.

When the day arrived, Father honoured his agreement and took us all to the City Hall. He escorted us into the hall and left. The atmosphere was electric. Everyone was singing along and screaming at the same time. You couldn't hear much for the screaming, but just being there was tremendous. I have never forgotten that experience. It made me even more determined that I wanted to sing pop music on stage. *That's my dream*, I thought. It was all I could think about.

Where can I find a group to sing with? I thought. I thumbed through every page in the newspapers and looked at all the advertisements. I also learned songs to audition with. At this time, Mr. Spinks, my singing teacher, approached me. He was organizing a pop concert to raise money for charity, and he wanted me to take part. I was so excited! Every week, during my singing lessons, we would learn new pop songs. Just before the concert, he taped me singing them. *My first tape!* I thought. I felt ever so proud.

I brought the tape home and played it for my parents. Mother didn't have a great deal to say. She shrugged her shoulders and said: "You're living in a fantasy world."

My heart sank, because all I wanted was some encouragement. Father looked at me and quickly said: "That was very good, your voice sounds like an Angel's." He stood up and put his arm around me. That made me smile. I loved my father. He had experienced disappointment in his life, and had to live with regret about not doing the things he'd wanted to do.

"Go for your dreams," he said. "You can only try and then you will see." That was all the encouragement I needed.

"Are you coming to the concert?" I asked him.

"Of course we're coming. I'll give you the money and you can get the tickets," he replied. The next time I went to my singing lessons, I picked up the tickets and gave them to my father. It was obvious that Father had said something, because Mother was a little more enthusiastic about the tickets and the concert.

I liked Mr. and Mrs. Taylor, our neighbours across the road. I saw them as my second family. When I asked them if they wanted to hear my tape, they were so enthusiastic and asked me to come straight away to their house. I played the tape for them and they were so excited.

"You are a wonderful singer! That is amazing!" Mrs. Taylor said.

"Can you get us tickets for the concert?" She asked.

"Of course I can!" I replied, filled with excitement.

The night of the concert, I was so excited about the stage, the lights and the people. Everyone was rushing around for last minute things. The orchestra was warming up and you could hear the murmuring of the audience.

"Five minutes, people," the stage manager said. My heart began to race. Just at that moment, a white light showed up and this angelic figure appeared. She looked at me and I felt this great calmness come over me. She was beautiful and held her hands open for me to walk forward. Then she disappeared. We rushed onto the stage, took up our positions and the curtains opened. There in front of us was the orchestra and the bright white lights. Beyond them, we could barely see the audience in the mist. The concert began and it was wonderful and that feeling of calm excitement stayed with me through the first two parts.

We had a break at the end of the second part, and I was singing solo to open the third and final part. During the break, I could feel the pounding of my heart and my mind started racing.

All these people are experienced professional singers, and here I am, a novice, I thought.

"Two minutes to your curtain call, Patricia," the stage manager called over the loud speaker. Sheer panic set in. I walked up the stairs to the stage and stood in the centre. At that moment, a white light appeared and the angelic figure emerged from it. I looked at her as the stage curtains opened. Everything seemed to be in slow motion. I felt my body floating and I looked down to see myself singing on stage. As I looked back, the figure and the white light had disappeared and I was back in my body, bowing to a standing ovation. It was an incredible feeling that I will never forget.

Who was that angelic figure? I wondered.

It's our experiences in life that make us who we are, a voice said. I turned around but no one was there. I stood by the side of the stage to watch the other people sing. They were professional singers who had beautiful voices. There was a tap on my shoulder. I turned and there was Mr. Spinks, my singing teacher.

He stood by my side and watched the other singers, and just before he left, he looked at me and said: "You have a wonderful voice. One day you could be professional, and better than these people. Just don't give up on your singing." Then he left.

The show ended and Father was waiting in the corridor.

"The show was wonderful, but the best part was you," he said, as he put his arms around me and walked me to the car. "I am so proud of you," he said quietly as we got into the car with the rest of the family.

Not a lot was said on the way home. I think Father wanted me to know things before we got into the car. He knew how things were between Mother and me. All the way home, not a word was spoken, so I stared out of the car window with my own excitement, looking up into the sky at the stars, wondering who my angelic figure was. When we got home, Mother insisted that it was time to go to bed. So upstairs I went, took my bath and got into bed, switching off my bedroom lights. I was so excited about the concert that I couldn't sleep.

As I lay in bed a voice said: *Remember, you are special, and you have a long way to go.*

"How would you know?" I asked, thinking that someone was in my room. When I looked, no one was there. The room lit up with bright light and the angelic figure appeared.

"Who are you?" I asked.

Before she could answer, my mother shouted: "Switch off your lights and go to sleep."

"Ok Mum," I replied. The angelic figure and the white light had disappeared and my room was dark once again.

My lights were off anyway, I thought. It seemed to take forever to fall asleep as my mind kept racing with the excitement of the show. That night, my dream was so vivid - about the show, the white light and the angelic figure. It was like re-living the experience all over again. When I woke up the next morning, I rationalized that my vivid dream was due to all the excitement.

The concert was the talk of the village for about a week. Mr. and Mrs. Taylor bought me a box of chocolates and told me how talented I was. They even suggested that I sing full time. It made me feel both happy and sad.

Why is it that Mr. and Mrs. Taylor can say these things, but Mother can't? I thought.

The only thing I got from Mother was: "If you think this concert changes anything you're mistaken. You're still going to get a proper job, with a steady wage," she said. This made my heart sad. I only wanted her to love me and be proud of me, but I never got either.

The excitement of the show stayed with me for a long time. There was a new spring in my step. Everyone I met over the next few weeks (who'd been to the show) stopped me, to tell me how good I was. I was with Mother one day when we bumped into Mr. and Mrs. Bowen. They said: "Your daughter is so talented. She should sing professionally!"

"Oh, she's going to get a proper job," Mother said.

"Well, if she were my daughter, I would want her to follow her dream. She could go far with that singing voice," Mr. Bowen said.

"Well, it's a good thing she's not your daughter, otherwise she wouldn't get anywhere," Mother said as she pulled away and walked on.

"Why do you have to be like that, Mother?" I questioned.

"Don't you start. All this has gone to your head, so you can just shut up before I smack you!" she said with anger. I knew it wasn't worth it, because she would have just gotten worse, so I kept quiet on the outside while inside, I mulled things over. I wished that, just once, she could be proud of me and show it.

That's a tall order! A thought shot into my mind from nowhere.

"Come on, stop dawdling," Mother said, pulling my arm. I never got the chance to explore those thoughts when my mother was around, because she always interrupted what was going on in my mind.

When I went back to school, the headmaster called me into his office. He had attended the concert and had enjoyed it very much. He said that my performance was good, and even better than some of the professional singers. His comment made me feel wonderful.

"Thank you sir," I replied.

"You've always been so musical, (singing in the choir and playing piano in assembly). What would you say if we did a concert of our own, with the choir and the school orchestra? You can sing the lead and solos. Then, we can raise money for charity!" he said, smiling.

"Oh that would be really good!" I said enthusiastically. *Another stage concert!* I thought.

"That's good then, we'll plan it, and you can be the star of the concert," he said as he walked out of his office. He turned back, looked at me and said: "We have a great deal of planning and practicing to do, don't we, Patricia?"

Divine Intervention

"Oh yes, sir, but it'll be worth it," I said.

"That's good to hear. Off you go now," he replied. I hurriedly walked to my classroom and never said a word to anyone.

The next day in assembly, there was a big announcement regarding the concert. It was so exciting. It created a great buzz around the whole school. Everyone began to talk about other ideas for raising money for charity, as well. This way, everyone could contribute in different ways. The headmaster sent letters out to our parents that informed them of what we were doing and asked for their help. For the next six months, everyone was planning different events. At the end of it all, came the concert.

The night arrived and the atmosphere was electric. My heart was pounding with both excitement and fear. The band was warming up and I could hear the people in the audience. It was absolutely amazing. We were assembled for curtain call and we all stood at the centre of the stage.

Suddenly, the white light appeared and the angelic figure came through the light. She was so beautiful. This time, she stayed with me for the whole performance (never left my side) and filled me with great calm and confidence. There were standing ovations of three minutes for each person after the end of the concert, and then the angelic figure disappeared. It was as if she was there to see me through, and when it was over, she left. She never said a word. She just looked at me with her kind, gentle eyes and smiled.

The school raised about £100,000 for charities over that six-month period. It was amazing how everyone worked together to achieve it. The concert was the talk of the school for weeks and teachers commented on my performance, saying how good I was. My parents also attended the concert, but Mother never said a word to me. I'd come to the conclusion that she didn't care, and I tried to convince myself it didn't matter – but it did.

When Mother was not around, Father said: "You were really good at the concert. While you were singing you could hear a pin drop – I am so proud of you!"

"Thanks Father, that means so much to me," I replied. He looked at me and smiled. Just then, Mother came back and he changed the subject.

Chapter Thirty-Nine

Journey to Atlantis

*B*eing given encouragement, especially when you're young, is so important. All I ever wanted Mother to do was to acknowledge that I had performed well at the concert. I'd sung my heart out, so that she, in particular, could hear. But it had no impact at all, and had fallen on deaf ears. I didn't understand her at all.

Why doesn't she like me? She wanted a boy when she had me, I thought. *Maybe it's that, or she just doesn't like me.*

I began to question. By this time, I had convinced myself that I was different and special, as my angelic beings had said. Those words helped me through these times.

My life could be so different, if Mother could only show me some love, I thought.

"You are loved by us all," a voice said.

"Who are you?" I questioned.

There was a pause of silence and then: "We are the spiritual beings from Atlantis," a female voice said.

Oh no, not this again, I thought.

"Don't be afraid, we will not harm you. We want to help you," the voice said.

"You're reading my thoughts!" I said out loud.

"Of course, we can read your thoughts, we have much to teach you," the voice replied.

"I don't want to go through this again, go away!" I cried.

Then, there was silence.

They've gone! I thought, and sure enough, nothing happened - just total silence.

I never dared ask the name of these spiritual beings, because I was frightened of them. *Are they good or bad beings?* I asked myself. *Am I really talking to myself? Are they devils trying to make me insane?* No one would believe that I was experiencing spiritual beings who talked in my head. I couldn't believe it myself, so why would others believe me?

I used to spend hours mulling over things, trying to determine whether it was all real or not.

One night, my dreams started again. Just at the point of questioning whether I was asleep or awake, I felt a heavy weight on my back. I was scared and couldn't move a muscle. I wanted to open my mouth and scream, but was paralysed with fear. Finally, I opened my eyes and saw myself hovering above my own body. A white light appeared and an angelic being came through the white light with arms extended.

Divine Intervention

"Come with me, I have lots to show you," he said. He held my hand and we moved through the white light. We travelled through time and space. It was like being at the cinema watching a movie. I saw wars, famine, different cultures and different countries as we flew back to a place he called *Atlantis*. The part about *Atlantis* was fascinating. It was like watching a film to learn about history. He showed me the whole of *Atlantis*: how it had been and how it destroyed itself. He told me of the crystal skulls and how they had been separated, so that no individual could have full power over all of the skulls. It was so fascinating and I felt so at home, a feeling that I had not yet experienced in my entire lifetime.

He brought me back through the white light into my bedroom, and before he left, he said: "*Atlantis* is where you belong. You were part of my family. For you, my name is Seth." Then he left and the white light disappeared. At that moment, I was awakened by the alarm clock.

All day, I thought of what had happened the previous night. *Was it a dream or was it real?* It fascinated me, because it had all seemed very real to me.

Over the next few weeks, the dreams kept happening: not every day, but every few days. Each time, I would take another journey to *Atlantis* and learn more. Then, after two weeks, the dreams stopped. My mind was constantly churning with all these thoughts of *Atlantis*. The burning question was: *Is Atlantis real?* I'd never heard of it in history lessons at school. So, was it real, or just a sequence of dreams I could never understand?

Chapter Forty

Father Finally Understands

*I*focused on my schoolwork and pushed those thoughts to one side, because I could neither prove nor disprove any of it at the time. To be honest, it was doing my head in. I wished I could find someone to talk to, but in the 60's a lot of what was happening to me was a closed book. No one talked about things like this. Mediums were doing the rounds at the spiritual churches, but no one openly discussed psychic things. *What could I do? Where could I go?* I didn't know.

My mother went to the spiritualist church with Father. At first, she went to help him, but later, it became something she did for herself. They used to go to *Open Circle*, where Father developed his abilities as a medium. He continued his training in spiritual healing and became well known in the South Yorkshire area where he appeared on platform with Harry Edwards. Father used to say that he felt very humble when he worked with Harry Edwards. Mother used to see things in her dreams, and eventually she found herself with psychic people, because Father used to visit a number of churches three or four times a week, doing his platform work and healing. Father used to work during the day, and then he spent his evenings doing things at, or for, the churches. My mother used to go everywhere with him, so eventually she became Father's little helper.

I couldn't find the space to talk to him alone about all the things that were happening to me. Sometimes, I would feel like shouting and telling everyone to go away, so that I could have some time with him. I was isolated and felt so alone.

When we were growing up, Father played the piano and we all joined in singing with my mother. We called them 'family concerts'. Father loved his music and liked to entertain us. We used to play charades and games instead of watching television. Father used to love to sit on the floor with the three of us and play card games: *Snakes and Ladders, Draughts or Monopoly*. We had some great family times while playing games and making up mimes. Mother used to go off and do things around the house while we played with Father. I miss those times.

We didn't have a great deal of money so we made our own toys out of all sorts of things. We also made up our own games to keep ourselves amused. Family life was important to Father. He would always take the time to play with us, both before his accident and after he recovered. Sometimes aunts and uncles would come with our cousins and we would have musical nights.

Divine Intervention

Mother had a lovely singing voice but never did anything with it. She would sing her heart out at the family musical evenings. Father used to say: "Your mother sings like an angel," and she would just laugh.

Mother was one of seven children and didn't have an easy life. She had diphtheria when she was young, and missed a great deal of school because of this illness. When she returned to class, she misbehaved and did not pay attention, because she'd missed so much and didn't know where she was, she was so far behind.

As a child, Mother was as strong as an ox and thought nothing of fighting the lads to stick up for her sisters. In fact, Father used to call me: 'Little Ada', my mother's Christian name. I used to get mad and say: "I am nothing like my mother!" and storm off.

I couldn't see any resemblance to my mother at all! But, perhaps I was a bit hot tempered and always fighting – just like her.

When I look back over my first fourteen years and my relationship with her, I find it difficult, because no matter what I did, I just couldn't please her.

She constantly compared me to my brother and sister, until I became resentful of them. They seemed to be able to get her attention and she acted as though they could do no wrong. I became the rebel and wanted to give her grief in return for her giving me a hard time. When it came to the three of us though, she would always stick up for us. If someone's parent came to the door and said: "Your Pat has been fighting with our Margaret," my mother would answer: "She wouldn't fight if she wasn't provoked, so don't come complaining at my house – look at your own daughter first!" She would slam the door shut, and then give me a hard time for fighting.

One Saturday, Mother had to go to town. The car had broken down, so she decided to take the bus. Father had bought a part for the car and was waiting for my brother, Terry, to finish work so he could help him with the repair. My sister went out with her friends, and that left Father and me alone in the house. I made him a cup of tea and brought it into the living room.

"Come and sit down, Patricia, I think its time to talk," he said.

"About what?" I asked.

"The things you can see – like at the funeral," he replied.

"So, come on now, we have time while everyone is out," he said looking at me.

"There are so many things I have seen," I said.

"Then tell me everything," he said, giving me an anxious look.

"I don't know where to start!" I replied.

"Stop going around in circles, and start at the beginning."

I told him everything that had happened to me that I could remember: Mother's relatives who had died; going to school and knowing what my classroom and teacher looked like before I saw them; the visions I had about the children at school; the events I had seen before they happened. I told him about the angels, the Guardian, the Brotherhood, the God-like figure, the events at the funerals, the travelling to places not of this earth, and of all the creatures or beings I had seen. I told him what had happened with the flying lights in my bedroom, all of the out-of-body experiences, and the dual realities. I mentioned the dreams, seeing colours around people, animals, birds, trees, plants and water, and described the faces I had seen in the sky, water, trees and bushes. My heart was pumping and my words just seemed to trip off my tongue, as though it wasn't me speaking.

This is another experience! I thought, as I suddenly looked down and could see myself talking to my father.

Within seconds, I was back in my body, talking to him again.

"You certainly have a lot to say!" Father said.

"Did you see anything, or did anything change while I was talking to you?" I asked anxiously, thinking he wouldn't believe me.

"Yes, Patricia, I did. I saw your angel and your voice changed," he replied with understanding.

"You believe me!" I said, excited.

"Of course, I believe you. I wouldn't see anything if you weren't telling the truth," he smiled.

"I'm so happy you believe me! I've carried this for a long time, thinking I was going mad!" I replied, stumbling over my words.

"You're not mad, child, you are gifted. It's just that nobody understands, because they aren't like you. They can't see and feel like you. In such a short life, you've experienced more than most people will in a lifetime. My healing and my gift as a medium came out of trauma. Your gift is natural, from birth. You know your Grandmother used to read tealeaves, so it runs in the family. Your mother and I used to wonder, when you were a baby, who you were looking and laughing at! You'd be looking in the opposite direction to us, and you'd be laughing and giggling, as though someone was there. Your mother put it down to wind, but she was so wrong!" he said laughing.

"Why does Mother hate me so much?" I asked.

"She doesn't hate you. She just doesn't understand you, because you're not the same as Terry and Angela. With them, everything is visible and normal - whatever normal is. You're so very different. You seem older than your years. You are intelligent. You have ambition. You always seem to know and have a perception of things. You see and experience things, where most people will never get the chance. Your mother is still scared of this. She's started having dreams and it unsettles her. She comes to churches with me because we have always been everywhere together. Your mother doesn't know how to handle all this, that's all," he explained.

"But how *do* I deal with it all? It's been bottled up inside for such a long time, with no one to talk to, and I'm not sure how to deal with everything that happens to me. I need some answers too, Dad," I pleaded.

"I know you do, and that's where I come in," he replied.

"But Mother won't let us spend time together to talk. She always barges in and splits us up!" I pleaded.

"Leave that one to me, Patricia. I'll sort it out. We'll get some time together every day, even if it's only half an hour," he said.

I loved and trusted my father with all my heart. He was special and my hero. His life hadn't been easy and he would still put others before himself.

Father once said to me: "There are so many people who need help in this world. We should do whatever we can to make a difference. So, never give up helping!"

I could have talked to him for hours, but Mother came back from her shopping trip and asked what we were up to.

"Nothing Ada, I'm just talking to Patricia," he replied. "You go out and play now Patricia, we'll chat later."

"OK, Dad, I'll be in the garden," I replied, as I got up and walked out. This was the start of another great powwow about me. *This could be interesting,* I thought.

Chapter Forty-One

Meeting My Mentor

*I*sat in the garden thinking. My Guardian, Grey Cloud, had told me that the time would come when my father would help me. This must be it. I couldn't be imagining those things that I saw. It seemed like I'd been in the garden for ages, when Father shouted: "Come inside, Patricia." My stomach was full of butterflies and my heart raced with anticipation. I wondered what they were going to say.

"It will be fine," a voice said. I looked behind me, but no one was there.

I opened the back door and slowly walked into the room with apprehension.

"Come on, sit down, you're not in trouble - far from it," Father said.

I sat down, still unsure of what was going to happen.

"I've been talking to your mother about what's been happening to you all this time. You and I will spend some time together each day to talk about things, and I'll explain things to you. Your mother agrees that I must help you," he said, looking at her.

"Why do you think I hate you, Patricia?" Mother asked.

"Because of the way you treat me and shout at me and take everyone else's side. I can't do anything right in your eyes. I feel like you wish that I had never born. You're always telling me that if your stillborn boy had lived, I wouldn't be here - that's why! I don't feel wanted or loved, and I certainly don't feel part of this family!" I cried, wiping my tears.

At that point, Terry walked in. "What's going on?" he asked. "Is she in trouble again?"

"Nothing is going on. She's not in trouble. Let's go and have a look at the car," Dad suggested, getting out of his chair and heading for the back door.

"I'm off to the fields for a walk," I said. I got up and left Mother sitting there in the armchair, silent. It was unusual for her to be silent, but she was immersed in deep thought.

I headed for my favourite spot in the fields by the stream. It was a lovely, sunny day, with just a gentle breeze. My heart felt better now that everything was out in the open, but the uncertainty of what would happen from here on was still in my thoughts. I sat down by the stream, looking at the sunlight flashing brightly on the water, wishing everything would blow over, and that some peace and quiet would enter my life.

"Aren't you happy?" a voice said.

I looked up and around, but there was nobody there. "Who are you? Where are you?" I questioned.

Out of the blue sky appeared the most beautiful being I had ever seen, full of serenity and the most peaceful calm, lighting up the sky with amazing colours.

"I am your teacher, Merlin," he said.

"You can't be Merlin – you don't even look like Merlin!" I replied.

"I am Merlin, come with me, and see," he said.

He held out his hand and I stood up, not feeling afraid. I held his hand, and in the blink of an eye, I was travelling the skies, going backwards in time.

This can't be real! I thought.

"Yes, it is real, Patricia," he said. "I am taking you back in time, to see the truth."

"But, I thought Merlin was a fictional character?" I questioned.

"You will see that I am not fiction, Patricia," he said knowingly.

Things were flashing before my eyes like watching the movies: wars, peace, famine & fires. People were changing with time. We hovered above an old castle, and then we went below the ground into a cave. The cave was full of old pots and lots of different stones (which I now know to be crystals), which seemed to light the place up. "This is my cave, where I did my work," he explained. "I am here to help and teach you, as you are going to be a great person one day, full of knowledge, who will help people overcome things and give them insight. Don't question it. Your father has opened the door, and I am here to teach you a little at a time."

He looked at me with calm eyes, then raised his staff and moved it around, chanting in some language unknown to me. A beautiful white light appeared and balls of coloured light (all the colours of the rainbow) flew through the white light. They zoomed to every corner of the cave and around my head.

I started to laugh, as I could hear child-like voices, giggling.

"Now you see, Patricia," he said.

"It was you who sent these coloured balls of whatever they are, to cheer me up when I was down!" I said excitedly.

"Yes, Patricia, it was," he laughed.

"This is amazing!" I giggled.

"You are my pupil and it is time now for me to help you on your path, so let's go back now," he said, waving his staff in the air, and chanting the unknown language. All the coloured balls of light flew back into the white light, and then they disappeared.

Within seconds, I was back by the stream and Merlin stood in front of me. "Remember, I am your teacher, Patricia," he said, and then he disappeared into the sunlight.

That was amazing! I thought, as I got up to walk home. I was singing as I walked, seeing, for the first time, how beautiful things were. The trees and flowers had vivid, striking colours. I'd never seen them like this before. Everything looked more vibrant and alive.

I was full of excitement when I entered the back door of our house.

"You're full of yourself, Patricia," Father said.

"I've just had an amazing experience with Merlin. He says he's my teacher," I said excitedly.

"Now that's going a bit too far!" Mother snapped.

"Come on Mother, don't be like that – the girl's telling you what she's seen," Father said to her.

"That's a load of rubbish, so don't you say anything to your brother and sister," Mother grumbled.

"So, nothing has changed – she still doesn't believe me. She always spoils everything for me!" I cried and ran off upstairs to my bedroom.

I could hear them talking in the living room and then footsteps on the stairs. My bedroom door opened and Father came in and sat down.

"It's going to take time, Patricia, with your mother," he said. "I believe you. This afternoon, I had a vision of Merlin and you, so I know you're telling the truth. Come downstairs and get some tea and we'll find time tomorrow to talk about it." He got up and held out his hand.

"Did you really get a vision of me and Merlin?" I asked, wiping the tears from my face.

"I did. We seem to be connected, and I'm seeing things that are happening to you. Merlin is showing me how to help you," he replied. "You know, Patricia, we have to keep these things between ourselves. Your mother doesn't know what to make of it, and your brother and sister are not ready to think reasonably. When your time is right, you will use your abilities. In the meantime, you have to be a young lady, and experience what you are meant to experience in your lifetime."

I took hold of his hand, and he gave me a cuddle before we walked down the stairs together. It made me feel a lot better, knowing that I wasn't imagining things, and that my dad could see things too. It felt so good to know that I wasn't going mad!

We all had our tea and then I watched TV, still thinking about Merlin, and what had happened that day. It was so amazing.

"Come on, Patricia, it's time for a bath and then bed," Mother said.

My mind was still full of Merlin and what he had shown me. It took me ages to drop off to sleep.

I got up the next morning feeling calm and serene. Father had already gone to work, so I quickly got dressed, ate my breakfast, and said goodbye to Mother on my way out to school. Everything felt different that day. There was lightness in my body and a feeling of joy in my heart. It was a *good-to-be-alive* feeling. I felt happy and the world looked different today, as if I had never seen it before, and exploring it for the first time. It was so colourful and exciting. I had found out that the one person I loved most was like me, and I could talk to him, because he could see what I could see. It was so wonderful to know that I wasn't alone in the world or going mad.

This is the first day of the rest of my life, I thought, filled with a new sense of wonder and understanding. I would never have believed I could feel like this. I wasn't a freaky kid anymore. I was a young lady (Father's words.) I had something that many other people didn't have, or would ever experience. It felt good to be different. A new sense of wonder filled in my life.

Dad was true to his word. We would sit down together every day, and spend time talking about my experiences.

Divine Intervention

The funny thing was, Merlin was there every time we spoke. We could both see him and when we finished talking, he left.

"Merlin is certainly your teacher Patricia. He's always here, giving me information to tell you. He says you're very special, and will do great things in your life. He's doing it through me, to prove to you that what you've experienced in your life is true, because I see it too," he said, with a gentle smile on his face.

"I feel privileged and humbled when Merlin is around, and with what I have experienced. Why can't everyone see what I can see?" I replied, questioning my father.

"Well, some people are meant to have these connections that you were born with, and Merlin explained some things to me. Since you've been little, you've always had an older head on your shoulders than your years. You've felt like an outsider, and you've always searched for something, though you didn't know what you were searching for. That's why you were born with spirit's wisdom. It's not an easy path, as you know Patricia, but you will achieve, later in life, all that you are meant to. Others come to things later, like me, and others will have lessons to learn before they can become whole and connected. Others may never learn from their lessons. Everyone is different in this world, Patricia, and as you walk through life, you will see there are plenty of people who will need your help. We all can't be the same, although we can all connect to our inner being, and bring inner peace to our lives. You will learn that not everyone wants to be helped. They may say the words, but never mean what they say, because they like being exactly where they are. Maybe that's their lesson in life," he said with a sense of knowing. The words just tripped off his tongue. I saw a white light and his voice seemed to change.

"That was your message from Merlin, Patricia, did you see things?" he asked.

"I saw a white light above your head, swirling around, and your voice changed. Your words just seemed to come out, without stopping, or pauses, as though you didn't take a breath," I replied.

"Now you know that Merlin is around you, and you've got your answer," he said calmly.

Father looked tired, so I thanked him, and left him to get some rest.

I went outside and sat around the back of the house. Our dog Bess followed and sat with me. The sky was so blue, not a cloud in sight, and the birds and butterflies kept coming nearer and nearer until I could almost touch them. They didn't seem frightened of me at all. It was as though they were comfortable and knew me. Things made more sense to me now. As I sat thinking, swirls of white light kept flowing around the garden. *It must be Merlin*, I thought.

"Indeed it is," Merlin said. "There is so much more peace inside of you, Patricia," he said.

"Yes Merlin, there is, I feel it and understand much more, thank you for helping me," I replied.

"I have to go now, as my time with you is at an end. Someone else will be sent as your teacher when the time is right. I will still be around and will watch you grow, but for now, my job is done," he said. He appeared in a beautiful cloak of many colours: purple, blue, yellow, red and green.

Divine Intervention

"Thank you Merlin, you really are my magician and you've changed my life. I'm so humbled in your presence, and words cannot express how you have made me feel," I replied.

"My child, it has been an honour. Remember, no matter what happens you are gifted and special," he said. His voice started to fade into the background and then he disappeared as he had come, in swirls of light.

I didn't feel sad that Merlin had gone, as I knew I would see him again one day when I least expected it. *He is only gone for now*, I thought.

Chapter Forty-Two

Becoming the Mentor

*M*erlin's help was monumental to me at that time in my life. Now, I have become the mentor myself. I sit here in my healing room, gaze at my crystals and marvel at the unusual experiences that I still have.

The more I meditate the more I get connected with my inner being and higher self. I have had some amazing visions including a painting that grew to the full size of the wall. The painting came alive and I could walk into it and walk out again.

I remember doing a reading for a young girl who was having a difficult time with seeing things. Her mother thought she was a mental case. She was so lacking in confidence that her questions were: "Am I really going mad? Will they lock me up in a mental institution (like my mother says) if I talk about things I can see?"

We talked for hours about what she was seeing and how her mother was treating her. She went home to think about everything we had discussed. Two weeks later she phoned and wanted to me to work with her and train her in meditation. She wanted me to work spiritually with her so she could understand what was happening and how she could control it and protect herself.

I put a training package together for her and introduce her to one of my work groups that includes people who are just like her. I bring her up to the group's knowledge before I introduce her so that they are all at the same level.

It was lovely to see her face that evening. It's like a light bulb turning on. "All these people are like me," she says with great relief.

She is introduced and made welcome by everyone. We have a cup of tea to allow everyone to get to know her. They talk about their experiences with spirit and their families.

Everyone is so interested in her story. She never stops talking as her face changes from one of caution to one of smiles. She is a chatterbox - like a kid with a bag of sweets.

Chapter Forty-Three

Leaving School

My father continued to help me by talking me through my experiences and telling me what he knew. It was good to know that I was not going mad. I had thought for many years that it was my nightmare, but now I could see who I was and why. What a relief!

I loved my father very much. He was always full of fun and we would play jokes on each other. He would chase me around the outside of the garage trying to get his own back. He was very special and thought of everyone but himself. It was great to have him back knowing that he knew who I was and what I had. Terry and Angela never knew about these things. It was kept between my parents and myself.

It was my last year at school and the headmaster called me into his office and said: "We are starting a sixth form next year to do O'levels. Would you like to stay on at school for another year?"

"I will talk to my parents when I go home and let you know tomorrow," I replied, leaving the room filled with excitement.

When I got home I was filled with joy, thinking I could study and go on to better things.

After tea, I asked my parents if I could talk to them about school.

"Come into the kitchen and we can talk there," Father said.

"You're not in trouble are you?" Mother butted in.

"No I am not" I replied, feeling angry.

"What is it Patricia," Father asked.

"Mr. Haigh is forming a sixth form at school for next year and he wants me to stay on and do O' Levels," I replied.

"You're not staying on. You're going to find a job and contribute to this family and that's that," Mother said sharply.

"Why is it always me who can't do something? I want to stay on and get O' Levels," I cried.

"You're not staying on. You are getting a job," she snapped.

"No Ada, leave the girl alone. She's ambitious and wants to get ahead," Father chipped in.

"I really want to do this," I said, wiping the tears away.

"You're not and that's that," Mother replied, waving her finger with anger.

"It's not that we don't want you to, Patricia, it's just

that we can't afford to let you stay at school another year," Father said, sympathizing with me. "I would love to be able to allow it but we just don't have the money," he continued.

"But, I have done so well at school and can do better. It's always down to money. I can make it up later," I pleaded.

"I wish it was that simple and that we could, Patricia, but we can't," he replied.

I ran out of the house and up the field to my spot against the stream, sobbing my heart out. I cried and cried until there were no tears left to cry with.

"What are you so sad about Patricia?" a voice asked.

I looked up and around but there was no one there.

"Who are you," I asked.

"I am Mathew, your teacher" the voice replied.

"I haven't talked to you before," I said.

"No, you haven't Patricia, but it's time for us to talk, he said.

"About what?" I questioned.

"You will have lots to deal with in your lifetime Patricia, and patience and humility are not easy lessons to learn," he replied.

"It's not just about you and you can't always have things when you want them. Sometimes, you have to wait until later," he continued.

"You're talking about school," I replied.

"Yes Patricia, I am. I'm a Buddhist monk and I know those things take time to happen. You will go on to study and find the discipline to study, but for now, you have other things to experience. Try to understand that you're parents can't afford to keep you at school. Think about how they feel right now," he said with conviction.

"We will talk again soon, Patricia," he said as his voice faded away into thin air.

He left me pondering his words as I walked down the field, heading for home.

As I arrived at the house and walked into the kitchen, I could sense an atmosphere that a big discussion had taken place.

Mother scowled at me. Dad looked at me with such sad eyes that I realized what Matthew had said made sense.

"It's ok, dad. I am disappointed but I do understand. I can study later. I have to experience things just now and that's ok." I walked over to give him a big hug.

"It's about time you saw some sense, lady. You need a job so you can start looking," Mother said with a negative tone.

"Leave the girl alone, Ada. She has thought it through so that's the end of it," Dad replied.

"I'm going to bed. I'm tired," I said, walking upstairs.

Life is strange, I thought. I loved my dad and I would not hurt him for the world. Although, I was disappointed, I realized that I was also being selfish and that was not good.

I got into bed and switched off the light. My mind was busy with thoughts of Matthew and how I was going to tell Mr. Haigh that I wasn't staying on at school. *What would I say and how would I say it?* These thoughts kept going around in my head until I fell asleep.

Divine Intervention

The next morning, I woke up and sensed that someone was standing over my shoulder. I felt a strong presence and smelled some sort of incense.

It must be Matthew, I thought.

"You are right, Patricia. I am with you to help you through today. You have learned quickly," he replied.

"I am glad that you are with me and that you will give me strength and confidence to do the right thing," I said.

"You have all those qualities, Patricia. I am here for support, that's all," he said and then, he disappeared.

It made me feel good that he was with me because my stomach was in knots.

I ran downstairs, ate my breakfast and just as I was about to leave, Mother said: "Don't forget to tell Mr Haigh that you're not staying on at school."

"I know what I have to do Mother. I don't need for you to remind me," I snapped, as I walked out and slammed the back door.

Why does she always have to be like that? I thought.

I walked to school and tried to work out what I was going to say to Mr. Haigh. The butterflies in my stomach grew stronger as I approached the school gates. I stopped for a while and thought about what to say, when suddenly a voice said: "Well, are you staying on next year" I turned around and there was Mr. Haigh.

"I would love to stay on Mr. Haigh, but my parents can't afford it. I have to get a job," I replied.

"Do you want me to have a word with them?" he asked.

"Oh, no sir, there is no need for that. We talked it

through last night and I do understand that they don't have the money to keep me at school. I will study later, probably at night school, while I'm working." I said with confidence.

"You are an interesting girl, Patricia, with a good head on your shoulders. You will do well regardless. I respect your decision. You are certainly older and wiser than your years and a selfless person as well." he replied, with understanding.

That felt good. *He respects me for what I've done*, I thought. That gave me a great deal of satisfaction and I felt a glow all day. It had been worth all the pain and tears because I felt good about myself. *I knew my parents could not afford it, so why put them under more pressure just to get what I want? I could do things later,*" I thought.

Several of my friends were staying on at school and they kept questioning me as to why I was not staying. "Because I don't want to and there are other things I want to do," I replied. I did not want them to know that my parents couldn't afford it. It was a small mining community and word spread fast, so I did not want my parents to be the gossip of the village.

Chapter Forty-Four

Earning My Keep

If I could not stay on at school or sing as a professional, then I want to be a hairdresser, I thought – a trade that would make my mother happy. So, I looked in the newspaper and saw an advertisement for an apprentice hairdresser at Mexborough. I phoned up and got an interview for the following Saturday. I had to take one parent with me.

Father said he would go with me. Saturday came, we went to the hairdressers for the interview and I got along really well with everyone there. It was a five-year apprenticeship. They offered me the job and told me to let them know on Monday. I really wanted this job but there was one snag. A £1500 bond had to be paid by my parents. They would get it back after I had completed the apprenticeship.

Divine Intervention

There was silence in the car. I knew my parents couldn't afford it and I knew that my father felt bad about it, so it was better to say nothing, even though my heart was filled with disappointment. There seemed no hope for doing what I really wanted to do. Everything I wanted required money, which we didn't have.

At this time, I felt abandoned by God, Angels, Spirit (whatever they were called) and lost my faith in them. For some reason, I could not move forward and do what I really wanted to do, so I pushed everything away from me having to do with Spirit.

What is my purpose in life? I thought.

"To help others," a voice said.

"Go away and leave me alone. I want nothing more to do with you." I cried.

The more they tried to talk to me, the more I pushed them away until one day there were no more voices and no further contact with them.

As my final term was coming to an end at school (with about two weeks to go), I came home one day and learned that my mother had been talking to the owner of the pet shop in the village who had mentioned that she was looking for someone to work there.

"I have arranged for you to have an interview on Saturday afternoon," Mother said.

"What if it is not what I want" I replied.

"You are going and that's that. You will have a job when you leave school in a few weeks time. I will take you myself and make sure you go and you had better make a good impression," she snapped.

I shrugged my shoulders and walked away. *A pet shop*

Divine Intervention

- I could do better than that, I thought.

Saturday came and Mother walked me to the pet shop, as promised. She introduced me, turned to me and said: "I will be back for you in an hour."

The lady was fine as she explained the job. There was a lot of lifting to do of heavy bags of all sorts of animal foods into the shop, cleaning the store and the animal cages – decorating the shop window (which I knew I would like) and cleaning the downstairs of the house (which I knew I would hate).

I smiled sweetly and afterwards, she said: "You have the job, Patricia. You can start in two weeks on Monday. Your pay will be £3.50 per week and you will work 9 am to 6 pm, Monday through Friday, with a half hour lunch break, and 9 am to 1:30 pm on Saturdays."

Wonderful, I thought. *I'll finish school on Friday and go straight to work on Monday.*

"Thank you very much and I'll see you then," I said politely.

This is awful, I thought, as I shut the shop door behind me. Even though I loved animals, I never wanted to work in a pet shop. I just wanted to sing. I was not looking forward to doing the shop cleaning and housework.

"Well how did you get on?" Mother said, grabbing my arm.

"I got the job," I replied, with sadness in my voice.

"There is no use being like that. You have a job and others don't. You will have money coming in, so don't be so ungrateful," she snapped, while tugging at my arm to slow down.

"But I know I can do better than this." I said, pulling

my arm free and running home.

Why do I always have to do as my mother says? She never thinks about what I want, I thought.

"A dead end job – that's great," I said.

"What's that you said?" Father asked, as I walked through the back door into the kitchen.

"Oh nothing," I replied.

"You don't look happy. Didn't you get the job?" he questioned.

"Oh yes, I got the job. Mother is making me take it. She won't let me find my own job," I cried.

"Just take it for now and look around for what you want. That's the best way to deal with it," he said, with encouragement.

"I'd never thought of it like that," I said.

Just then, Mother walked in. "She's an ungrateful child" she snapped.

"Now then Ada, it's just not what she wants but she's going to take it until something better comes along," he said.

"So she should," she muttered under her breath.

I walked outside and sat in the back garden, dreaming of far away places and anything else to help me stop thinking about the pet shop job.

Leaving school for me was a sad occasion. I loved learning. I had a curious mind but knew that I had to leave school and start working. Everyone there said their good byes and I walked the last walk home from school, feeling like I was grown up and starting work to earn some money. It wasn't what I wanted to do, but what I had to do.

As I got in from school that Friday night, it was as

though it wasn't real, but a dream. Monday would make it a reality.

I made the most of my last weekend before I started work and spent a great deal of time walking up the fields and sitting by the stream contemplating my future.

If only I could leave home and make my own decisions. I could do what I wanted to do, I thought. Life was meaningless unless I could do the things I wanted to do and explore my own potential to grow.

I felt lost without Spirit around me but I was determined not to have anything to do with my supernatural acquaintances. *What was the point of being guided through life if nothing would go right? I was being knocked about at every turn. Surely, things were not meant to be like this, if you're being guided along your way. It's all a load of nothing – a waste of time! I don't believe in anything anymore. What was the point?* I thought.

I had taken our dog, Bess, with me on this day and she was lying down beside me.

I looked down at her and said: "Why is it my life is so difficult when it is so easy for others? Maybe one day, I will show the world that I am *Somebody* and then my parents will be proud of me." Bess sat up and looked at me with a sense of knowing, wagged her tail, licked my face and then cuddled into me as though she knew that's just what I needed. I put my arms around her and cuddled her, with tears running down my cheeks. She kept looking up at me and licking my face. I just knew she could feel my pain.

We stayed by the stream for a while and then walked slowly back home. I had an affinity with nature and animals that I never understood. All I knew was that nature and animals made me feel much better.

When I got home, I went to sit in the back garden and my father came to join me.

"You look so sad, Patricia" he said.

"Oh, I am just thinking about my life and what has happened and where I am going. You know, starting this job is not what I want to do but I know I have to do it," I replied.

"Sometimes, we have to do things we don't want to do until something better comes along," he said putting his arm around me and giving me a cuddle.

"I know Dad. It's just disappointing. I had so many dreams," I replied.

"I know Patricia, but you can still go for your dreams. Never give up on those dreams. Go for what you want whether it works or not and then you will not have any regrets in life. You can at least say that you've tried," he said, with disappointment in his face.

"Why? Do you have regrets?" I asked.

"Yes, Patricia, I have. I had chance to go into business with someone but your mother and I talked and she wanted a wage every week and the security of that, so I did not bother. My instincts said to do it but I went against them to please your mother. You can't turn the clock back. You only have one chance. So no matter what anyone says, you go with your instincts and go for your dreams. You will make it in life. You'll see at the right time and you'll look back on this time as a learning experience that has made you grow," he answered. Then he got up and went back into the house.

Divine Intervention

This gave me food for thought. *Maybe my dad is right. I will go for my dreams,* I thought.

Monday came and I got up early to get ready for my first day at work. I had my breakfast and left the house to make sure I arrived early.

I got there about 8:50 am and waited for the shop door to be unlocked. I heard the bolts being removed and the door opened.

"It's lovely to see you Patricia. Are you ready for your first day?" Mrs. Smith asked.

"Yes, thank you." I replied.

Mrs. Smith showed me how to work the till and the weighing scales and she went around explaining what all the foods were and what to do and what not to do.

The first week went fast and Mrs. Smith gave me my first week's wage. I felt so excited that I had earned some money. When I got home from work, Mother was waiting in the kitchen.

"Come on, hand over your wages like everyone else," she said holding out her hand.

She took my wage packet opened it and took the money out.

She handed me 10 shillings and kept £3.

"What's this?" I questioned.

"Three pounds is for your board and 10 shillings is for you to buy clothes or spend as you like," she snapped.

"Is this all I get?" I asked.

"Yes, and that's an end to it," she said with anger in her voice.

I stormed off and thought: *Why work if that's all I get.*

I was so mad but there was nothing I could do. *I just*

can't wait to leave home, I thought.

Over the next couple of weeks, Mrs. Smith stood in the shop and watched me to make sure I understood everything and then left me alone to make my own routine.

I loved decorating the shop window every week and serving the customers. I did not like cleaning her room and the shop.

The time seemed to fly by.

I got along with her daughter, Carise, who was about seven years old. When she was off from school, she used to help me and we would spend time playing with the animals. She was an only child and felt alone. I think that's why we both got along so well.

Carise had a cat that she used to dress up in baby clothes. It used to run around the house and the shop all dressed up. It was such a soppy cat. As soon as she dressed it, it would stand on its claws, hiss and run frantically around the house expecting you to chase it. Carise used to make me laugh with that cat. Mrs. Smith made me like feel part of the family. Her husband had died and they were on their own running the business.

While I was there, they went away and left me to look after the shop. It was the first holiday they were able to take in a long time. She asked a relative to drop by to make sure that I was ok and to see if I needed help, but I managed fine.

About two months after they came back from their holiday, Mrs. Smith called me into the living room. She didn't look happy at all. So, I had a bad feeling.

"Sit down Patricia," she said, patting the seat next to her.

Divine Intervention

"You know that you are just like a daughter to me and you are part of the family. Carise loves you to bits as well. I couldn't ask for a nicer, harder working or more reliable person," she said.

"Thank you" I replied.

"I don't know how to say this, Patricia, but," she said pausing.

"But what?" I asked.

"I have to let you go because the shop is not paying its overhead and I can't afford to keep you. I may even have to sell and move," she said, with great sadness in her heart.

"I am sorry to hear about your troubles. I have loved it here but I do understand," I replied.

"You're a good girl, Patricia and I do wish you every happiness and success. I am giving you an extra week's wage and your holiday pay so you can have time to find something else," she said.

"You don't have to do that if you need the money. I would rather you have it," I replied.

"No, Patricia you are a kind-hearted person. I want to do this for you because you deserve it. I am just sorry to lose you. I know someone else will benefit from my loss so if you need a reference, just ask," she said, as she got up to lock the shop door.

"You can go out the back way," she said, as she turned and walked away.

There was so much sadness in her voice. I knew she was crying, so I walked out the back door and headed home.

In one way, I felt sad because they were lovely people

and I had enjoyed working for them. In another way, I felt relieved because now I could find something else that I wanted to do.

When I got home, my parents were talking in the living room.

"Hand over your wage packet," Mother said, holding out her hand.

I handed over the packet without saying a word.

My mother opened it as usual and counted the money.

"What's this? There are two weeks wages," she said.

"Mrs. Smith had to let me go because she couldn't afford to keep me on. She may have to sell the shop. She didn't like doing it but she had to," I replied.

"You've done something wrong," Mother snapped.

"Why is it that you always think I've done something wrong? I haven't," I cried.

"I will find out for myself young lady and whoa be tide to you, if you have," she said with anger.

"Well you just do that Mother and we will see who's right, won't we? Let's see who has to apologize," I said and walked off into the kitchen muttering: "I hate this house."

Mother kept her word and didn't care whether or not it was Sunday. She was determined to prove that I had done something wrong.

When she came back home, not a word was said.

"Well, Mother, had I done something wrong?" I questioned.

"No, and don't expect an apology either," she snapped.

Mother never liked to be wrong and didn't take it

very well when she'd obviously made a fool of herself.

Maybe this would give me a chance to change direction and do something I want to do, I thought.

I started looking for work and got an interview with a firm of solicitors at *Wath-Upon-Dearne.* It was a receptionist's job with some typing and it would give me a chance to meet people, which I loved.

I got the job and started right away, which surprised my mother. This time, I had chosen my job and that made me feel good. I settled in very well and within a month the solicitors said: "We have never had the telephone system handled so well and the reception service as never been so good. Nothing is too much trouble for you. You always have a smile on your face and a very pleasing personality. Our customers keep making good comments about you, so we are very pleased with you and your work, Patricia."

Those comments made me feel special. Finally, someone had recognized the good in me.

I loved the job and knew that I was doing well because the solicitors kept giving me more and more responsibility regarding typing. I would fly through the work and always produced a good standard of quality that everyone recognized. I was happy and content with my job.

This surprised my mother because I think she expected that I would get bored. What she could not take away from me was the fact that I had gotten the job on my own and had put my heart and soul into it. I was even paid more money.

This rekindled my ambition to succeed in life.

Chapter Forty-Five

Falling in Love

When I was fifteen, my brother, Terry, went on a holiday with some college friends to the Norfolk broads. When he came back, he said: "One of my friends (Trevor) plays the guitar and his band is looking for a singer. I mentioned you and he wants you to go for an audition if you are interested."

"Oh yes, I am interested," I said, full of excitement.

"I will see him on Tuesday, so I will set it up for next Saturday," he replied.

"She's too young for all that band stuff," Mother chipped in.

"Oh, let her have a go. She can sing! Why do you always try to spoil things?" Terry snapped.

Mother huffed and walked out of the room.

It came as a surprise that he stood up for me, but I

knew that he had been experiencing some of the same comments from her and had enough of her negativity.

On Saturday, I caught the bus to Barnsley. Terry had shown me a picture of Trevor so I would know who to look for at the bus station.

The bus pulled in and there was Trevor, waiting at the bus stop. He was a tall, thin, shy guy about four years older than me. "Hello Patricia. It's nice to meet you. I'm going to take you to the rehearsal room," he said.

"Nice to meet you," I replied.

"Terry, has told us about your singing, so we thought we would try you out and see what happens," he said, as he walked me to his car.

"That's fine," I replied.

The conversation was a bit stilted on the way. Trevor was quite shy and I did not want to chatter away and appear stupid.

We stopped at a local school and went in the back to a workshop. There were four other 20-year-old males with guitars, keyboards and drums, just jamming out.

"This is Patricia," Trevor shouted and they all stopped playing and walked over to introduce themselves.

"Shall we try a few songs Patricia?" Trevor asked.

"Yes, that's fine," I replied.

It was the sixties and *The Beatles, Dave Clark Five, Kinks, Cilla Black, and Lulu* were all popular. We played a number of songs and the time just flew by.

They all wanted me to join them and do more rehearsals on the weekends because everyone was working. After about three months of rehearsing, we got our first gig on a Saturday night.

Divine Intervention

Mother wasn't very happy (as I was just sixteen) but Trevor convinced her that they would pick me up and drop me home after the show. She did not object because Terry said: "Let her have a go and don't be so obstinate, Mother." So, she let me go.

It was great to be on stage and know that I could entertain. It had always been where my heart was. Mother couldn't complain because I had my day job during the week and I sang on the weekends.

I really enjoyed myself and every time I sang, I saw my angel who was so beautiful. It was as though she was a part of my singing. She never said anything but just directed a bright white light down upon me. It made me feel so good.

Over six months, we played many gigs and were also the backup band for the *Dave Clarke Five* when they appeared in Barnsley. Life appeared to be good. The band had lots of fun and after the shows we used to play 'ten pin bowls.'

Over this time, Trevor and I became close friends. We both liked music so our interests were the same. He played guitar and I sang. For once in my life, I had someone who loved music (like me) and who wanted to be a musician. We spent a great deal of time on our own just talking about our music, hopes and dreams. He knew everything about me and never forced me to do anything, so I felt comfortable and safe. He never rushed me. It took him six months to find the courage to hold my hand and kiss me. So when he finally did, I was not scared.

I didn't know what love was meant to feel like because I had never felt it before. He made my heart pound and my body tingle. The passion felt so real and I felt alive for the first time in my life. *This must be love,* I thought. It felt like Cinderella going to the ball and meeting her Prince Charming for the first time. That first kiss was the start of our relationship. He took me to Blackpool and proposed on the beach. I was still sixteen at the time and had to ask my parents for their permission.

When I got home they were still up, so I decided it was then or never.

"Trevor proposed to me today and wants to get engaged now and plan the wedding," I said in a hurry with butterflies in my stomach.

"You're too young to get married," Mother snapped.

"I just knew you would spoil it for me," I cried and ran upstairs to bed.

I could hear loud voices downstairs and knew the conversation was about me.

I thought: *She will always have control over my life.* Then, I cried myself to sleep.

That night I had a vivid dream (in full colour) of me walking down the isle in a white wedding dress and veil.

When I woke in the morning, I could remember every detail.

I went down stairs to find my parents sitting at the breakfast table. Mother was unusually silent.

"Your mother and I have talked and you can get engaged as long as the wedding is after your 18th birthday," Dad said.

"That's ok dad, I'll tell Trevor," I replied.

Trevor was all right about it. He bought me an engagement ring and we had our family and a few friends over to celebrate.

Chapter Forty-Six

Accelerated Wedding

I was very young and had experienced so much hurt and disappointment in my life that it was not easy for me to just fall into someone's arms and say: "*I love you.*" All I knew was that Trevor made me feel so different inside and I looked forward to being with him. During that time, Trevor and I had a full relationship.

Mother had never given us any sex education so I didn't understand anything except my periods. I was very naive.

Then one day, I took a pregnancy test after missing two periods. The bomb had dropped: I was pregnant.

This is going to go over like a lead balloon, I thought.

I had to work up the courage to tell my parents because I was not yet seventeen. With great anticipation, I waited for the right moment to tell them. One night, when

I came home, they were sitting in the living room and I just blurted out: "I'm pregnant."

There was no response so I headed for the stairs door.

"You're pregnant?" Father asked.

"Yes," I replied, feeling anxious.

"How would you know," Mother snapped.

"I'm not stupid. I've had a test done at the doctor's office," I snapped back.

"You'll have to get rid of it and have an abortion," she said, with anger in her voice.

"I am not having an abortion! You always want to hurt me, don't you?" I cried and ran upstairs to bed.

My heart was beating faster and faster and I cried until I couldn't cry any more. At that time, my angel appeared through a white light and gently said: "Don't worry Patricia, it will be all right." Then, she disappeared.

That night, I slept like a log and woke up in the morning feeling that something was about to change.

I went downstairs and there was my father and mother, just looking at me.

"If you want to have this baby, Patricia, you had better start making some wedding plans," Father said with a gentle voice.

"We can't afford a big wedding but we can sort something out.

"Thanks dad, I'll tell Trevor," I replied.

Trevor and I decided that it would be a September wedding. I would be seventeen in June and it would give us time to find somewhere to live.

The wedding caused arguments because his family

wanted a big wedding and my family couldn't afford it. His family even wanted to pay for the reception so that they could have what they wanted.

I knew that this would hurt my mother and father, so I said "No." It would be my parents who would organize the reception. Trevor and I nearly broke up because of his family's interference. We finally came to a compromise: we would get married in Barnsley and hold the reception in Thurnscoe. There was a great deal of stress around the wedding plans. Trevor and I argued one night and I ran off, fell on the pavement and landed on my stomach. He came running and picked me up but the pain had started in my abdomen. He took me to hospital where I had a miscarriage.

Trevor had to phone my parents because they were keeping me in hospital overnight. He took me home the next afternoon.

He stayed awhile at my house and then left to go home and get some rest. Afterwards, I was sitting in the living room with my parents. No one said a word, so I went to bed.

About four days later, I was in the house with my father when he asked: "Are you all right?"

"Yes Dad, I'm ok."

"You know, you don't have to get married if you don't want to. We can postpone it, if that's what you want to do."

"It's all right Dad. I'm ok with the wedding as planned," I replied.

"Are you sure that's what you want to do? If you need time to think about it or if you change your mind, we won't be upset," he said.

Divine Intervention

"Yes, Dad, I'm sure the wedding can go ahead," I said anxiously.

I walked into the garden thinking: *What was all that about? Maybe he just doesn't want me to get married.*

The wedding plans carried on and Trevor and I looked for a place to live. We found a cottage to rent in *Denby Dale*. This meant that I would need to get a transfer to another office in *Wombwell*, which I did.

My sister, paid for my wedding dress and my mother organized everything for the reception.

When my wedding day arrived, I put on my wedding dress and walked down the stairs, where Father was waiting for me. Everyone else had left for the church.

"You look beautiful, Patricia. You are a beautiful young woman and I am proud to be taking you to church. I have just one question: Are you really sure that this is what you want to do? It's not too late to stop everything," he said.

"It's ok, Dad. What's wrong?" I asked

"I just want to know that you're making the right decision and that you're going to be happy," he said, with sadness in his voice.

"I'm fine, Dad. Come on! I'm getting married today so we should be happy," I replied, trying to make him smile.

The car showed up and we walked out of the front door. All the neighbours stood in the street, shouting and cheering.

"I feel famous," I said.

Father laughed and said: "Well it is your big day. You're the first of my children to get married."

It was a long journey to the church in Barnsley and

we were quiet. I knew that I would not be going home tonight and he knew it also. I could feel his sorrow.

We got to the church and he walked me down the aisle. The long train to my wedding gown flowed behind me. I felt like a movie star with everyone staring and I could hear the comments regarding how beautiful I looked. It felt like a dream that I would never forget.

After the wedding ceremony, we headed back to Thurnscoe for the reception. His family was a pain because they tried to spoil everything. I quietly pulled his mother to one side and said: "Either you shut up or leave because you are not criticizing my parents. They have done what they could afford which is better than what you would have done. I have had enough of you and what you are doing. The choice is yours: I can announce that you are leaving or you can sit down and shut up."

She never said another word for the rest of the reception. Our guests seemed to enjoy themselves and then we had to go to our new house that was a two-hour drive away.

We said our good byes, I threw my bouquet (which my sister caught) and we headed for our new home.

I was still in my wedding dress as we drove off. We were both quiet because it had been a hectic day. When we arrived at our new home, Trevor carried me over the threshold and we started our married life.

I was so happy. It felt like a dream. I had a husband and a home. What more could I want? I could laugh and be myself but, at the same time, I was also scared that someone would take my happiness away. I loved to cook, so I would make all my own food: bread, cakes and all sorts of meals.

Divine Intervention

I became the housewife that I thought I would never be. I worked, kept our home nice, clean and comfortable. This felt so good to me. I had never been so happy. For the first time in my life, I felt like a real woman.

Chapter Forty-Seven

Living with the In-Laws

Within a few months, the journey to work became difficult because of the weather and it ended up being a long one for both of us. At the same time, Trevor's car became unreliable and, without consulting me, he asked his parents if we could move in with them. They agreed.

I was furious because I did not want to live with them, but what alternative did we have? We moved in and I was so unhappy. We had a bedroom that was too small for privacy. I spent more time with his family than he did because he managed to work late to keep out of the way.

I became pregnant within a couple of months and that did not help either. His mother was an interfering busybody and I could not stand her. I was determined to stay at work for as long as I could because I was not going spend more time with his parents. I was also going to find somewhere else to live before the baby was born.

Trevor changed his job and ended up working in *Goldthorpe*. I was fed up with looking at houses and then, doing nothing about them. We had seen a new house in *Thurnscoe* and it was £2,175.00.

We just needed the deposit, so I phoned up Mr. Stone and asked him if he would lend us the deposit, and we would pay it back each month. He agreed, so we bought the house and moved in.

We didn't have a lot of money. We had no carpets and just a few second hand bits of furniture, but it was our home and I was so glad that we were on our own.

I was eighteen that June and my daughter, Angela, was born in August. She had a natural birth.

I did not know what to expect because my mother did not tell me anything. Although, I was young and inexperienced in these things, I did what I felt was right.

We were short of money so I had to find a job. My mother was against me going back to work. She would not agree to look after Angela so I could earn some money. So, Trevor asked his parents if they could help out. They said 'yes' because Angela was the first girl born into their family.

Every day, Trevor would get up early, take Angela to his mother's house and pick her up at night. After a couple of weeks, he came home and told me that he was dropping her at his mother's on Monday morning and picking her up on Friday evening. I was furious because I had no say in the matter. They had convinced him to do it so they could have her most and influence her life.

Divine Intervention

I was stuck between a rock and a hard place. I had to work because we needed the money but I couldn't find anyone else to look after her so I could have her back each day.

My heart sank more each day. I was so unhappy without my daughter. They would be the first to hear her first words and see her walk. *How could Trevor do this too me?* I thought.

It was a hard struggle to pay our bills, even with two salaries. Trevor kept buying furniture on finance and our bills kept increasing.

Eventually, his parents decided to buy a shop at *Goldthorpe* so that they could have their own business. I thought this would make my life easier with Angela closer, but not a great deal changed. Trevor would never stand up to his parents. They just wanted to hang onto my daughter, no matter what.

We only had one car. I worked at Thurnscoe and would walk across the pit fields to their shop at Goldthorpe to get Angela and bring her back by bus.

This caused great arguments between his parents and me. I was crying and my 'so-called' husband would not do anything to retrieve Angela from their clutches.

Trevor came home one day and told me that I had to work in the shop because his parents needed help.

"They will pay you for helping," he said.

"How much?" I asked.

"I don't know, but it's got to be better than what you're getting now, so you can give them your notice," he said.

I would do anything to be with Angela during the day, so I went to work the next day and gave notice that I was leaving.

Divine Intervention

Everyone at work told me not to go. My friends said that it was the worst thing I could do, because Trevor's parents would have control over me. I didn't listen, because I just wanted to spend time with my daughter.

I did not want to be with his parents but I so wanted to be with Angela. I prayed to God each night that everything would be all right.

Once I had given my notice at work, I began working at Trevor's parents' grocery shop.

I hated it. I was their slave while they sat in the living room and watched television. Then, they would walk into the shop and say that I had not done things properly or that I was slow. I bit my tongue for a while to keep the peace for Angela's sake. I just wanted to be with her.

Each day, it got worse. They not only controlled my daughter, but they controlled me, putting me down until one day, I snapped.

Trevor's mother was having a go at me for no reason. I shoved her up against a wall, grabbed her clothes around her chest, lifted her up off the floor, put my face about two inches from hers and shouted: "You keep doing this to me and I will break every bone in your body! Do I make myself clear?" I dropped her to the floor and she scurried off to the living room to tell her husband.

He stepped gingerly into the shop and asked: "What do you think you're doing to my wife?"

I ran up to him, grabbed his clothes around his chest, lifted him up off the floor with one hand and asked: "Why? Do you want the same treatment? I am sick of you both. You can stuff your job and this shop." I grabbed Angela and headed for the door.

"You can't take Angie! Trevor said that she has to stay here," he said.

"Do you want to try and stop me?" I shouted as I walked out, slammed the door behind me and headed home.

When I got there, I bathed Angela and put her to bed. Trevor was still at work, as usual.

About 7:30 pm, a car pulled up outside. Trevor's older brother came to the door. I opened the door just as he arrived.

I never liked his older brother, because he was arrogant and very smarmy.

"What do you want?" I asked.

He pushed his way inside saying: "I heard you upset mum and dad"

"Have I? That's interesting," I replied.

"Well, I'm not here to talk about that," he said, as he moved towards me.

"Get away from me. You creep!" I snapped, as I pushed him away.

"You know you want me," he said in a creepy voice.

"I would not touch you with a barge pole, you creep. Get out of our house!" I shouted, pushing him away.

He ran toward me, put his hand over my mouth (so I could not scream), pushed me to the floor and ripped my clothes off with his other hand. I kicked and fought him as hard as I could. He ripped my knickers off, unzipped his trousers, pulled his penis out and tried to force himself inside me.

I tried with all my strength to push him off me, wriggling my body to get free. He pushed down on the front of my body and that gave me a chance to free one leg. I pulled my knee up and pushed him over, kneeing him in the groin.

He released me and rolled over in agony. I jumped up, grabbed the phone and called the police.

"You get out of my house now. You sick bastard, or I will press the button to ring the police – your choice." I was disgusted and filled with contempt.

"I said get out! Do I make myself clear?" I snapped in anger.

"I am going," he said, as he got up, straightened his clothes, walked out of the door and slammed it behind him.

I watched from the window to make sure that he had gotten into his car and drove away.

My heart was pounding. I quickly ran upstairs to see if Angela was all right. She was sleeping soundly and had not heard anything. Relieved about that, I took a bath and changed my clothes. I felt dirty and sick to my stomach.

When Trevor came home from work, I was still in a bit of a state. I told him what had happened with his brother. He went off the deep end and shouted: "You are a liar. It must have been your fault or you must have encouraged him. My brother would not do anything like that. He is married! You are sick and you need to see a doctor. I don't want to hear another accusation against my brother."

"I did nothing and did not invite him here," I shouted. "I did not want him here and I can't stand him. He is an awful person," I cried.

"How could you take his side? I'm telling you, that's exactly what happened. Why don't you believe me?" I asked.

Divine Intervention

"He wouldn't do that! Get your act together and stop making up stories," he snapped, as he walked out, slammed the door and drove off.

I cried for over two hours. *No one believes me. I am so unhappy,* I thought, as I walked upstairs to go to bed.

Since getting married, I had not had a connection with Spirit or the Angel. Life had been busy in different ways.

I had my studies, a daughter I adored and my job. I had even let go of my singing because I just could not do everything.

Friends were limited and even when they visited us, Trevor would go upstairs and not come down until they had left. They often would ask us out but he never wanted to go anywhere.

I was a friendly person and liked people around me, but all I had was isolation and four walls. Life seemed unbearable. I was in a bad situation again with only Angela to hang onto.

Trevor stayed out more and more and did not come home until 11pm. I cried and felt like life was not worth living. I was twenty years old and so unhappy.

I had such a bad time with Trevor's parents trying to control my daughter and me.

I had left the shop and found other work as a supervisor in a sewing factory. They were keen to train and promote me but most of the money I earned was going to pay the debts that Trevor had run up. After that, there was not a great deal left. I always made sure that Angela was well dressed and had what she needed. I, on the other hand, had very few clothes. After some time, I was forced to make a decision..

Divine Intervention

I had to take Angela back to Trevor's mother during the day. I had no one else to rely on because my mother refused to look after her. I worked hard and made sure that I would pick Angela up from his parents' house every night, no matter how tired I was. I just wanted her at home with me. Trevor had decided to start his own car mechanic business, so I saw even less of him. He was not earning a great deal of money and he insisted on renting another place to work from. We lived mostly off what I earned. I did not mind but money was very tight.

My twenty-first birthday arrived and I made sure that I had party - no matter what! I could not celebrate my 18th birthday because I was 7 months pregnant and looked like a beached whale.

I arranged for a baby sitter and Trevor and I went off to the clubhouse and met my parents for a meal. There was music playing so I danced all night. I had lost a lot of weight since the birth of my daughter. Hot pants were in and I had the figure to carry it off. My hair had grown fairly long and I felt really good at the party. Everyone told me how great I looked. I don't think Mother was impressed with me showing off my figure because I was married with a child and I should look 'like a mother'. The expression on her face said it all that night. But nothing was going to spoil my evening. I had a good time and was sad for it to come to an end.

Everyone said good night and we set off for home. There was total silence in the car. Trevor never said a word.

"Do you have to spoil my birthday?" I asked.

"Birthdays are irrelevant. There's nothing special about your 21ˢᵗ birthday," he said.

That was it for me! I could not take any more and we argued all the way home.

As the car stopped outside our house, I said: "Well, thanks ever so much for such a great birthday! Why is it that you always have to spoil everything?"

"I don't want you to have a good time. I want you to suffer," he replied, getting out of the car.

I walked into the house, said good-night to the baby sitter, and sat alone for a while in the dark.

While I was sitting there, a big white light appeared in the living room and a huge Angel appeared in blue and green.

"Are you Raphael?" I asked.

"Yes, my child, I am," he replied.

"Why is all this happening to me? I can't take it any more!" I said, bursting into tears.

"In the next few months, you will not be in this situation. You'll see," he said as he disappeared into the white light.

Chapter Forty-Eight

Sadness and Heartbreak

*I*sat reflecting on my life. Here I was, twenty-one years old, and what a life I had lived. Still, I was unhappy. When I looked back to meeting Trevor, I realized that I was not in love. He helped me feel something at that time that I did not get from my mother. I know now that I married him just to get away from home.

I went to bed feeling sad. That night, I had the most powerful dream in full colour, which I remembered when I woke up. It was about Trevor. I saw him in his garage and people were demanding money from him. I also saw him leaving the garage in daylight and going to this house. When the door opened, a young woman came to the door and threw her arms around him and they stood at the door kissing and cuddling with such passion. I felt so much pain. I could not believe my eyes. At this point in my dream, I woke up.

Divine Intervention

All day long, I questioned my dream and had a bad feeling inside. It was Sunday. I was home with Angela, studying for a management course, when a knock came at the door.

I opened the door and there were two large men who looked like heavies (nasty pieces of work).

"What do you want?" I questioned.

"Are you Trevor's wife?" they asked.

"Yes," I replied.

"Your husband owes us three month's rent on the garage and says he can't pay. He said we could have as much sex as we wanted from his wife to pay the debt." Then, they pushed their way into the house and grabbed me.

"You can go to hell!" I shouted, kneeing one of them in the groin. I managed to free my arms, grab the phone and quickly dial the police.

"Get out of my house NOW, or the police will be here in five minutes," I shouted.

The police answered the call: "Hello?"

"Just one minute," I said.

"Are you going?" I asked the men.

They walked out, and I said: "Don't you ever come back here!" and slammed the door.

I quickly ran back to the phone and said: "Sorry, I had a bit of trouble with two men who would not leave my house, but they are gone now."

"Are you all right?" the officer asked.

"Yes, officer. I am. Thank you," I replied.

"If there is anymore trouble, just call us," he said.

"Thank you, I will," I said, as I put the phone down.

I'm sure the officer heard my voice trembling, I thought.

My heart was racing and I felt sick, but had to see to my daughter who was crying from the noise of loud voices.

I grabbed her and hugged her so tight. Tears were running down my face.

How could Trevor send these people to our house when he knew my daughter was at home? I questioned.

The thought of what could have happened to Angela scared me so much. Here was her own dad doing this and anything could have happened. *He obviously doesn't care about either of us,* I thought.

Once I had calmed Angela down, I sat with a cup of tea. I felt like I could tear Trevor's heart out. Then, I remembered my dream.

The first part had turned into reality, I thought.

The second part was about my husband having an affair. I sat and pondered this one.

He's never home, comes in late, never eats with us and we do nothing together as a family, I thought.

I decided that I would wait up for him that night and confront him about the day's events.

11pm came and I was so tired that I could not wait up any longer. So, I switched all the lights off and went to bed.

Although I was tired, I couldn't get to sleep because my mind was working overtime. About midnight, I heard the front door open. It was Trevor. He stayed downstairs for a while and then came upstairs. Thinking I was a sleep, he got into bed.

For a few moments, I didn't say anything.

Then suddenly, I asked: "What's all this about you owing money for the garage and sending men around here to have sex with me to pay the bill?"

"I hope you had sex with them," he replied.

"You must be joking! I called the police after a struggle. How could you do that to me and know that your daughter was in this house? You're not a father. You are pathetic!" I cried.

He jumped out of bed, grabbed me and pulled me to the floor, putting his fist to my face.

"You had better do it the next time they come around or I will make you regret it," he shouted.

With his anger oozing out and his face in the moonlight, he looked liked a monster. *This wasn't the man I married*, I thought.

"I won't do it. I will call the police. You will just have to pay your debt another way," I said, kneeing him in the groin.

While he was doubled over in pain, I ran into Angela's bedroom, (she was crying), shut the door and cuddled her. I stayed with her all night, afraid of what might happen. I never slept a wink, just in case. I was determined to make sure that Trevor would not come in and do anything.

When the adrenalin kicks in, you don't care about your own life – it's about survival. The only person I cared about was my daughter and I was sure nothing was going to happen to her. Even if I had to lose my own life in the process, I was going to take Trevor (and his thug friends) down with me.

I heard movement about 5 am, so I lay quietly as though I was asleep. The front door slammed shut. I quickly jumped up to the window and peeped from behind the curtain to make sure he had gone. I watched him get into his car and drive away.

Thank goodness he's gone for now, I thought.

I quickly got both of us up, washed and fed. I had a plan. I phoned work and said that I had a problem. I then phoned a friend who came around with her husband straight away. They knew something was wrong and they also knew that I was psychic.

When they arrived, we talked about what had happened and about my dream. Anne's husband, Mick, was hopping mad and he wanted to go and beat up Trevor. Anne stopped him and said: "That's not going to help. We need to find out what he's doing first."

"You and your daughter can come and stay with us a few days while Mick finds out what he's up to. That way you will be safe," she said.

"Ok, I'll take a few days off work," I replied.

I phoned work and then quickly packed some things for both of us. I left a note for Trevor saying that we'd be away for a few days and then went off with my friends to their house.

Trevor didn't know about these friends so he would not know where to find me.

Mick took time off work and got a few of his friends involved to follow Trevor and see what he was up to.

It was good to have some peace and quiet and have a friend to talk to.

I used to go to my parents whenever Trevor and I fought, but never let on that anything was wrong. My father used to ask: "Are you all right, Patricia?"

Divine Intervention

And I would reply: "Yes Dad, I'm just tired with working, studying and looking after the family. I just have a lot going on."

He used to look at me as if he knew, but never said anything.

I didn't want to burden him with my problems and I knew what my mother would say: "You got married and you have a daughter. You have to stay with him no matter what." So, I never said anything.

My father was a medium, so I knew that he knew, but he left it to me to tell him, which I respected him for.

After a few days, Mick came home with a couple of friends and some photographs.

"We thought we would get some photos so there would be no mistaking anything and so you would have proof of what we had seen," he said.

We all sat around the kitchen table with a cup of tea. There in front of me, were pictures of my husband with another woman, holding hands, kissing and some interesting pictures of sexual activities in the car and in the woods, etc.

My heart sank and I started to cry. Anne jumped up and put her arms around me.

"What are you going to do, Patricia?" she asked.

"I just don't know. My mother is difficult and old fashioned and I know she will not want me to leave him – but I am sure I cannot stay either," I cried. My heart was in so much pain.

Mick and his friends decided to leave and give us some space.

You don't have to decide right now. You can sort it out later.

She changed the conversation and tried to make me laugh to cheer me up, but my mind was racing.

Another part of my dream had happened, I thought.

I sat there thinking of the Angel Raphael and what he had said about me not being in this situation much longer.

Just then, Mick returned home by himself.

"Have you decided what to do, Patricia?" he asked.

"Leave the girl alone," Anne said.

"No, it's all right, Anne. I'm fine. I have decided that I'm going to leave Trevor and divorce him. I can't stand it anymore. I am so unhappy."

"Where are you going to live?" Anne asked.

"No matter what, I am going to have to go back home to my mother and father and work it out from there. I'll just have to put up with what happens there for awhile," I replied, with a sense of calmness.

"When are you going to do it?" Anne asked.

"Tomorrow" I said, with great determination.

"Well, you're not going back to that house by yourself. I am coming with you," Mick said.

"What's the plan then?" Anne asked.

"You look after Angela tomorrow morning and Patricia and I will go to the house in the van and pack up what she wants," he replied.

"There is no need for the van. I am just packing up a few clothes for us both and some of Angela's toys. That's all I want. The rest can be sorted out with the solicitor," I said.

"Ok then. We'll get an early night and be fresh in the morning," Anne said.

"What time does Trevor go to work?" Mick asked.

"Usually, he leaves about 7 am," I replied.

"Then, we will go about 8 am, just in case he's late for any reason," he said.

"OK," I replied.

That night, after I had put Angela to bed, we sat, had a drink and talked about my situation. I enjoyed being there with them and it was good to have friends to talk to.

My heart and head were in turmoil and my stomach was full of butterflies, just thinking about what I was about to do. *How will I survive?* I thought.

Ten o'clock came and we all went to bed so we could be fresh in the morning.

I couldn't sleep a wink all night with thoughts running through my head. *What will my mother say?* I kept thinking.

A knock came at the bedroom door and Anne came in with a cup of tea. "It's six thirty Patricia," she said.

"Thanks Anne."

I got us both up and ready and we went down for breakfast.

"Are you going to ring your parents?" Anne enquired.

"No. I will just show up. That way, my mother can't stop me from leaving with nowhere to go," I replied.

"Are you ok?" Anne asked.

"Yes, I'm fine. I will feel better when it's all over and I am at my parents house and the arguments have stopped," I replied.

"Come on Patricia. We best get going. It's nearly 8 am," Mick said.

I got up, put my coat on and headed for the door.

"See you in a short while Anne," I said, as I left the house.

When we arrived at my house, Mick went inside and looked around to make sure that Trevor was not at home. He came to the front door and waved at me to come in.

It was strange going back into the house knowing what I was about to do, and that I would never see my home again.

Mick stood guard by the front door while I packed. When I had finished, he loaded everything into the car and we drove away. I looked over my shoulder at the house for the last time. It was a strange feeling. It was like someone had just died and I was grieving, but I knew it had to be done.

We went back to Anne's house and she made each of us a cup of tea. Everyone was silent while we drank our tea at the kitchen table. We didn't look at each other. Angela was playing in the living room and we could here her chuckling now and again. Mick got up and peeped around the door to see what she was up to and laughed as he walked into the living room to play with her. I think he just wanted to leave the two of us alone.

"Well, someone seems to be enjoying herself," Anne said.

"Yes, it doesn't take much to amuse her," I replied.

Then, there was silence.

What would my parents have to say, I thought.

I knew that my dad would be all right but my mother would be difficult.

"Are you ok?" Anne enquired.

"Yes," I replied.

"You seem miles away," she said, putting her hand on mine.

"Just thinking of what my mother will say. I know my dad will be ok, but my mother is a different kettle of fish," I said, with a feeling of anguish in my voice.

"I am sure it will be fine," Anne said, trying to give me reassurance.

"I'm sure it will, but it's probably better to arrive after dad's home from work," I replied.

"That's fine. When does your dad get in from work?" Anne asked.

"Between 4 pm and 4:30 pm. So, if I get there about 5 pm (after he's had his dinner) that will be about right," I replied.

But in my heart, I knew it was not going to be simple or straightforward, especially with my mother.

"Right. That will give us time to do some things and keep busy. In fact, I will pack some food and drinks and we will all go to the park," Anne said getting up.

I put some things together for Angela and we all piled into the car and went to the park.

Mick was very good with Angela and took her on the swings and roundabout and even sat her on his legs and took her down the slide. She laughed and giggled as we watched.

"She's having a great time, but I think Mick is having a better time," she said laughing.

They couldn't have any children of their own, but if they had been able to, they would have been great parents. Mick was like a big kid and enjoyed playing games with Angela.

My mind was in deep thought. My stomach felt as if something had died inside with the anxiety of knowing that I had to face the wrath of God from my mother.

Anne could sense my feelings and said: "Everything will turn out all right, you know. Just wait and see."

"I know that I've made the right choice. I will just feel better when its all over with my parents so I can sort myself out from there," I replied.

Time passed so quickly.

"We'd better get Angela off the swings and head back to our house to get things sorted out," Anne said.

I laughed as Anne shouted for Mick to bring Angela and head for home.

"I was enjoying myself," he said, with a sense of disappointment in his voice.

We all got into the car and drove to Anne's house. It was 4 pm.

"We have time for a cup of tea and a rest before you have to go," Anne said, as she organized things.

I helped, but said nothing as that feeling of anticipation was setting in even more. The butterflies in my stomach were turning into great big knots. I was dreading what was to come but I knew it had to be done.

The next hour lasted a lifetime. Every time I looked at the clock, it seemed like it hadn't moved.

"It's been only a minute since you looked at the clock the last time," Anne said with a smile.

"I know, but I am dreading it," I replied.

"Let's have a game of cards to take your mind of things," Anne said as she placed the cards on the table.

We played cards until 5 pm.

"Come on Mick, it's time to take Patricia to her mum's and dad's place," Anne said.

"I'm coming," he replied.

We all piled into the van and drove to my parent's house.

As we pulled up outside, Anne asked: "Do you want us to come in with you?"

"No, it's better that I do this alone," I replied.

I got out of the van and Mick helped carry my stuff to the door. I got hold of Angela and turned and looked at Anne.

"Thank you for all you have done. I won't forget it. You are a good friend," I said with tears in my eyes.

"You know where we are. Give me a call tomorrow. Let me know how you are and how things are going," she replied.

"I will," I said as I walked down the driveway to the back door.

I passed Mick going back to the van.

"Keep your chin up," he said.

"I will," I replied.

As I walked to the back door, Mother appeared.

"What's going on?" she asked, with suspicion in her voice.

"Let me get inside and I will tell you," I replied, pushing my way past her to get inside before a scene was made on the doorstep.

Chapter Forty-Nine

Moving Forward

*M*y life was like that – doing things that had to be done. Never in a million years, did I ever dream that my experiences as a child would help thousands of people. But looking back with the maturity of my years, I now have the knowledge and understanding that prepared me for who I am today: a spiritual teacher and trainer, a coach and counsellor, a medium and a healer who helps people through their fears, emotions and traumas. I help them change unwanted life patterns and move them onto their right pathway to create inner peace and a happier and brighter future.

Like many counselors, I know that we are in a special place and time. To help others grow and develop, in ways they cannot see for themselves, makes us truly humble. We have to experience far more than most in order to be able to help those in need. Our experiences make us who we are and allow our souls to grow and evolve to unforeseen heights.

Divine Intervention

We may be different but we are also unique. We can't always see why things happen to us at the time they happen, but we understand later that these experiences occur to help us grow, learn and prepare for the future.

Like many of my clients, I used to feel like I didn't belong to anyone, anywhere or even on the planet. My visions helped me, but I also feared what I could not understand. I felt so lonely and isolated. I lacked confidence and self-esteem. Many times, I felt like ending my life because I felt so frightened. I so desperately wanted to be wanted, understood and loved.

But as the years went by, I had to be willing to face myself and look deep within - not just say the words because words alone had no meaning.

I had to take action to find what was within my heart and mind. I had to be able to face and deal with whatever came, no matter what. That was the only way to find inner peace. I have now brought my soul home to a better place.

In that monumental move back home, with Angela in my arms, I found myself again questioning: Would my relationship with my mother ever improve? Would she ever really love me? Would I be able to show my daughter, the love that was never shown to me? As I grew older, I would learn the answer to that question, in ways I would never expect.

Photos

Grandmother and Grandfather at Blackpool

Grandmother and Grandfather at Blackpool

Mother and father at the beach

Mother and father with dog - Bess

Patricia as a baby with brother and sister

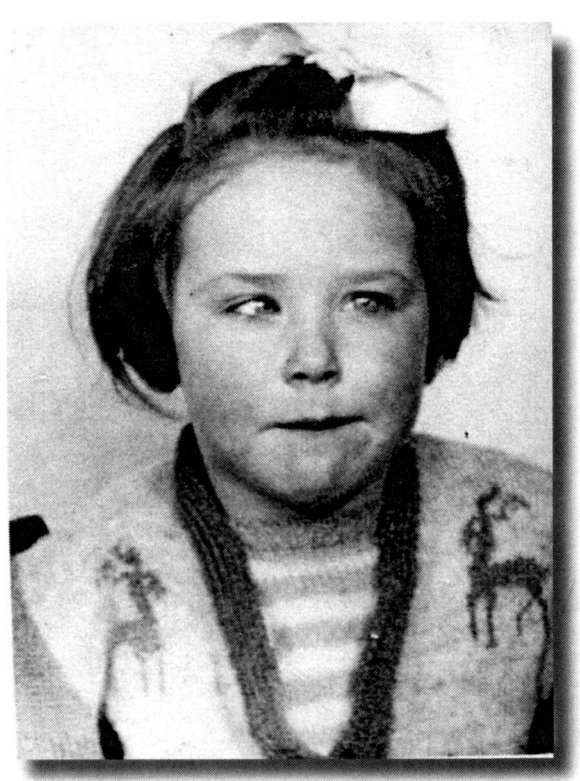

Patricia - Age 5 - with Lazy Eye

Patricia - Age 7 – with brother and sister

Patricia, seated in chair, Front Row Center

Patricia, seated in chair, First Row, Second From Left

Patricia - Age 16 - On Stage

Patricia – Age 16 – Near Waterfall

Patricia with her father on her wedding day

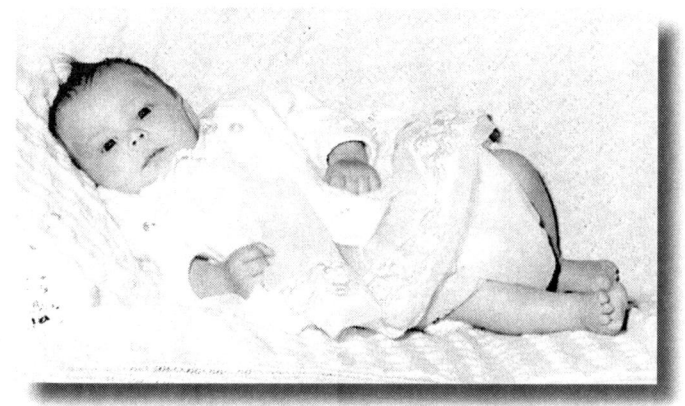

Daughter Angela as a baby

Patricia with daughter Angela

Patricia with daughter Angela at the beach

Patricia with daughter Angela

ABOUT THE AUTHOR

Patricia Milner is an International Psychic Medium, Reiki Master, Spiritual Teacher and Trainer who has been psychic since birth. Professionally, she has worked as a Human Resource Director and later managed her own Human Resources business. For the last ten years, she has worked full time in the counseling, training and healing fields.

In her current practice, she uses crystals, crystal energy, colour, sound and sound vibration to help people heal. Her spiritual retreats guide people through life's challenges and help them with their spiritual growth and development.

Patricia has written articles for national magazines and was a contributing columnist for a local newspaper in England covering topics on Spiritual Well-Being. She has also appeared on numerous radio and television programs discussing her work.

Visit Patricia's websites at:
www.patriciamilner.com
www.yourspiritualworld.com

Printed in the United Kingdom
by Lightning Source UK Ltd.
134628UK00001B/76-120/P